Guilt-Free MOTHERHOOD

Parenting with Godly Wisdom

DR. JULIANNA SLATTERY

FAITH
COMMUNICATIONS

Health Communications, Inc.
Deerfield Beach, Florida

www.hcibooks.com

Scripture quotation is taken from *The Holy Bible New Version*©, New York International Bible Society, 1978. Used by permission.

Library of Congress Cataloging-in-Publication Data

Slattery, Julianna, 1969–
  Guilt-free motherhood : parenting with godly wisdom / Julianna Slattery.
    p. cm.
  ISBN 0-7573-0226-2
  1. Mothers.   2. Mothers—Religious life.   3. Motherhood—Psychological aspects.   4. Parenting.   I. Title.

HQ759.G854 2004
248.8'431—dc22

                                                                        2004054215

Faith Communications (FC), its Logos and Marks are trademarks of Health Communications, Inc.

Publisher: Faith Communications, Inc.
          An Imprint of Health Communications, Inc.
          3201 SW 15th Street
          Deerfield Beach, Florida 33442-8190

R-10-05

Cover design by Andrea Perrine Brower
Inside book design by Lawna Patterson Oldfield

What People Are Saying About
Guilt-Free Motherhood . . .

"It is my privilege to recommend Dr. Slattery's book. It will encourage any mother who is struggling with guilt and feeling overwhelmed—and isn't that every mother at some point? The book was an inspiration to me as a mother and as a professional. I appreciated her insights on parenting with godly wisdom and focusing on how God builds us up as mothers through the task of motherhood. This book helps us take our eyes off ourselves and our own efforts, and focus instead on our Savior."

Judge Brenda Burnham Unruh

This book is lovingly dedicated to my mother, Jo Rybka.

Mom, you have no reason to ever feel guilty! You unselfishly devoted your life and energy to glorifying God as a mother. Thank you for all you have invested and continue to invest in us. You are my teacher, my mentor, my dear friend.

All my love, now and eternally!
Juli (Your birthday present from God)

"Her children stand and bless her. Her husband praises her: 'There are many virtuous and capable women in the world, but you surpass them all!' Charm is deceptive, and beauty does not last; but a woman who fears the Lord will be greatly praised. Reward her for all she has done. Let her deeds publicly declare her praise." Proverbs 31:28–31.

CONTENTS

Part III: So, What Do I Do with My Guilt?

ACKNOWLEDGMENTS

As I think about the process of writing this book, I am overwhelmed by the number of people who have encouraged, advised and instructed. Many have contributed their unique gifts and perspectives to make this an effective instrument for moms.

Special thanks to Peter Vegso, Lori Golden, Allison Janse, Kathy Grant, Bob Land, Lawna Oldfield, Andrea Brower and the rest of the HCI family. Thank you, Debbie Prinz, for your marketing genius and John McPherson for allowing me to use your brilliant illustrations. Thanks to Jon and Marci Bucciarelli for your courage and for sharing your story for God's glory.

Thank you, family and friends, for reading all or portions of the manuscript along the way: Mom and Dad, Wendy, Cheryl, Warren, Amy, Steve, Angela, Pam, Kim Bush, Anne Volk, Christie Orosz, Pam Knight, Stephanie Massa and Susan Beebe. Special thanks to my good friend Susie Sartarelli and the rest of the

Riverwood guilt-free mothers who volunteered as guinea pigs. Thanks, Ellen, for keeping me on my toes!

Thank you, Dr. John Coe, for teaching me to love wisdom.

God has so richly blessed me with parents who honored God throughout parenting and beyond. Thank you for your love and excellent example! God has also blessed me with you, Mike, my teammate in parenting and life. I am so grateful for you. Although they don't know it, my children have contributed mightily to this effort. Michael, Andrew and Christian: I thank God for you and I pray that this book does not put undue pressure on you.

FOREWORD

In 1989, I was invited to speak at a secular women's conference in Anchorage, Alaska. The topic was family issues and I was the token conservative speaker. The front row was full of women proudly wearing their NOW (National Organization for Women) buttons.

When I finished my talk and stepped off the platform, I was swarmed by a dozen furious NOW women, telling me that my approach to family was outdated. At the same time, another woman worked her way through the horde of women, got right in front of me and then turned around. I will never forget what she screamed at the women from NOW.

"You have lied to the women of America," my defender began screaming. "People like you tried to convince us we could have it all and do it all. But I've only lost it all! You told us we could have wonderful careers, beautiful homes, exciting marriages and great children. I am in a mediocre law practice, back living in a tiny apartment, and I have lost my marriage. Worst of all, my children are suffering and I have to share them on weekends. I've made a mess of everything!"

With that she collapsed into a sobbing heap and the women from NOW walked off in silence. Without meaning to, this woman opened the door to the real topic of need for these women: guilt. The rest of the day was spent in impromptu discussions about parental guilt. Some ladies had large issues of parental guilt, while others talked about things that seemed so insignificant. Being the only male observer in the building one thing was obvious: The vast majority of these ladies were walking around shackled by maternal guilt. It was amazing listening as the guilt poured out. I began feeling guilty about not having my own parental guilt.

As a man, I had never realized how prevalent and powerful the emotion of guilt was for women . . . especially in the area of motherhood. It is not only powerful, it is also very debilitating. If not handled properly, guilt can drain the energy out of a mom. It can also extinguish the fires of her parental creativity. Worst of all, guilt can make her feel like a loser as a parent—so much so that she can find herself looking elsewhere to meet her self-esteem needs.

A mom can never possibly anticipate and prepare for all the circumstances that each child will encounter. It is only natural to try to be or supply everything the child needs. But this messianic complex only leads to failure and guilt. Only God can meet all the needs of the child. Mom is simply a primary vessel. It is important to know that God loves our children significantly more than we ever could. As mothers process and discuss this truth, the chains of guilt will fall away.

Julianna Slattery, a mom, a professional and a Christian, has finally given moms a book that dissects this topic of guilt. More specifically a book that will help moms everywhere shed the bondage of parenting by guilt. This book offers mothers the freedom to have fun raising their children as a ministry for Christ rather than as a drudgery in the chains of guilt.

Dr. Robert Barnes
President, Sheridan House Ministries

INTRODUCTION

A few years ago, someone suggested to me that I should consider writing a parenting book. My response was, "How can I? My children are not grown." It seemed outrageous to write a parenting book while in the thick of motherhood. There were so many trials I was yet to experience. And what if my children didn't turn out well? Wouldn't it invalidate my message?

Now I sit in front of my computer completing a book I never dreamed I would write, at least not now. My children are seven, five and one, all boys. I am not a seasoned pro at motherhood but a fellow sojourner. I share many of your questions, fears and joys as I raise my children alongside you.

For me, writing this book has been a remarkable exercise in faith. It would be a lot safer for me to wait twenty years, look back on my failures and successes and teach from those. It's not difficult using hindsight to figure out how to parent. More challenging is finding truth in the midst of motherhood. I am confronted daily with my own inadequacies, limitations and mistakes. Often I wrestle with fear and guilt. Am I doing a good enough job?

I know that God desires that His children parent with confidence. That assurance can't come from our own understanding, the advice of others or even good intentions. It must be the result of our daily dependence upon God and our hunger for His wisdom.

Psalm 119:105 says, "Your word is a lamp to my feet and a light for my path." For mothers, the path is often dark. We don't know what tomorrow holds. We can't see the final result of our parenting. The advice of experts may be helpful, but only the Word of God can keep us from stumbling.

This book is not intended to give you my advice or wisdom, but to point you to the light that I am seeking in motherhood. Just like you, I wake up every day with messes to clean up and decisions to make. I change diapers, pack lunches, break up arguments and hope for naptime to last just ten more minutes. My confidence in writing this book is not based on my own parenting, but my faith in God's promise to give wisdom to those who seek it.

No book, including this one, can possibly exhaust the topic of motherhood. Some aspects of parenting are not addressed. One obvious exclusion is the role of your husband in parenting. As I meet with women in counseling, I see so many variables that affect the mother-father dynamic. Some are married to caring, involved men. Others are married to workaholics. Still other women are married to men who are critical or even abusive to their children. Half of women are no longer married to the father of their children. I wanted this book to address all these situations. Therefore, the focus is exclusively on a mother and what she is doing with *her influence*.

The title *Guilt-Free Motherhood* may also be misleading to some. If you are hoping to instantly feel good about motherhood by glossing over mistakes and imperfections, then you have picked up the wrong book. Guilt-free motherhood is not easy. It requires a lifetime commitment to seeking God through the journey of motherhood. God promises to purify us and free us from guilt, but this promise is conditional on our relationship with Him.

This is not a how-to book. Rather than telling you what to do, I hope to challenge how you think. A single mother with four teenage daughters has drastically different circumstances than a mother of a five-year-old autistic son. The parenting advice for each would be different. However, God's wisdom is available and effective for all mothers. Godly, faithful mothers come in all different forms. Some love to bake and play, some like to run a tight ship, and others scrape by with just enough energy to make it through a day. However, they all have one thing in common: They seek the Lord through motherhood.

Every morning, you face many challenges. Some of them are common; some are unique. The wisdom that God offers and promises is up to the task. Our Father wants you to parent guilt-free, with full confidence in Him. He is greater than your past, your weakness and your fears. Journey with me as we seek His strength and wisdom as mothers.

Part I

Why Do I
Feel So Guilty?

And the
Verdict Is . . .

Michael, our first child, was three months old. I had suc-
cessfully maneuvered the initial months of motherhood
and now felt like an expert at changing diapers without getting
squirted, bathing him, relieving his gas pain, buckling him into
a car seat and singing lullabies. One week, I began to notice a
dramatic decrease in the number of messy diapers my son was
making. Not that I missed cleaning the mustard diapers, but I
called the pediatrician to make sure everything was okay. My son
had gone four days without a BM. Was that normal? The doctor reassured me that breast-fed babies often produce little waste.
The days of poop-free diapers extended to twelve. I became very
concerned and took my bundle of joy into the doctor's office.
When they put him on the scale, the nurse informed me that
Michael had lost a significant amount of weight since his last

visit. "Your body doesn't seem to be producing enough milk for him. Your baby has been undernourished for the past month."

As a young mother I panicked. I burst into tears on the way home, begging my little Michael for forgiveness. "I am so sorry. I have been starving you!" All of my perceived victories as a new mom evaporated into one big failure. I felt so inadequate! This was my first vivid encounter with what I then knew would be my constant tormentor as a mother: guilt.

As I walk through daily life as the mother of three young children, I am constantly reminded of endless opportunities to feel guilty. It seems that everywhere I turn, my shortcomings are evident. I cannot do everything perfectly. I often feel overwhelmed. I lose my temper. I am embarrassed by my children's behavior, and I am baffled by my own inconsistency.

As I talk with other mothers, both socially and in my practice as a psychologist, I see that they, too, battle the ever-present shadow of guilt:

- ♡ Your child's friends can all recite the alphabet, but not your little girl. What are you doing wrong?
- ♡ You read an article reminding you that kids need at least four to five servings of fruit and veggies a day. The only ones your child will go near are ketchup and French fries. Are you setting your children up for future health problems?
- ♡ At a parent-teacher conference, you learn that your ten-year-old daughter is goofing off and not completing homework assignments. The teachers suggest that maybe she has

attention deficit disorder and you should consider giving her medication. Did you let your daughter watch too much television as a child, and why didn't you notice her problems earlier?

♡ You pick up your son from Sunday school to learn that he has punched a fellow classmate. Where is his self-control?

♡ You arrive home from having dinner with a friend to find your son with an enormous bandage on his head and scrapes on several other body parts. He had fallen out of a tree while you were painting the town. Would he have been hurt if you were home to protect him?

Moms with young children are not the only ones to feel guilty. Many mothers don't even feel a reprieve from guilt when their children turn into adults. It may seem that everywhere a mother looks she can see how her faults have damaged her children. I have met with many mothers of adult children who regularly agonize over how their mistakes may have set their children up for pain and failure.

"Maggie just won't stand up for herself. She's been walked over and taken advantage of her whole life. I should have been a stronger role model or encouraged her to be more assertive. I feel so responsible for the abusive relationships she gets into. And now it's hurting my grandchildren!"

Why do mothers struggle with such guilt? Although fathers may have some regrets and fears for their children, mothers seem to be consumed by them.

When she is handed that precious child, every mother is struck with the reality of how much this fragile life depends upon her. *I can't believe they are letting me take this baby home!* she thinks as she and her baby are escorted from the hospital. She must feed, clothe, bathe, comfort and love this little one, or no one will. Even if she has been around infants before, her first moments of motherhood are filled with a new appreciation for how enormous this responsibility is.

As infants grow into children, children into teens and teens into adults, a mother's understanding of her responsibility only becomes greater. A seven-year-old doesn't need her diapers changed, but she needs direction and comfort in dealing with relationships and rejection. A fourteen-year-old boy may be capable of basic self-care, but he needs his mother's loving direction to navigate through the fears and challenges of adolescence. Suddenly the memories of changing diapers and midnight feedings seem simple compared to the challenges of parenting this developing child. *If only his problems were that simple again,* moms lament.

With each new stage of development come a handful of opportunities to experience failure. For example, when my oldest son started school, I certainly didn't anticipate a battle with guilt. Having spent twenty-four years of my life in school, I didn't think twice about the transition. Boy, was I in for a rude awakening! Being a student is much easier than being the mother of a student. I was forever forgetting which day was show-and-tell, losing field-trip forms and sending him to school out of dress code. The worst of it was that school presented the opportunity for my mothering to be compared with all of the other mothers. While some moms brought in homemade cookies formed in the shapes of the alphabet, I sent in Oreos. I could hardly manage to keep carpooling days straight while it seemed that other moms knew the names of all the kids in the class.

The culmination of my "kindergarten guilt" came when Michael's class was putting on a teddy-bear play for the school. Each mom was told to make a bear costume for her child to wear in the play. I can't even sew a button on right! The night before the costumes were due, I scrounged through the closet and found an old Winnie the Pooh costume. Unfortunately, it was two sizes too small. "Wait! There is also a Tigger costume just Michael's size. This looks sort of like a bear." I sent it to school with him. When I picked Michael up, he had his Tigger costume with him. "Michael, why are you taking your costume home when the play is tomorrow?" Michael informed me, "My teacher said I can't wear it. She asked another mom to make me a bear costume."

Since that day, I have had nightmares that my son will fail kindergarten because of something I forgot. Sure, I could get a doctorate, but I can't get my kids out of preschool. As inconsequential as my teddy-bear failure was, it struck a chord with the deep fears of my inadequacies and the effects they may have on my kids.

While many of the mistakes we make end up being innocuous, what mother doesn't worry that her failures and shortcomings will harm her kids? One mother told me that she is not only saving for her children's college but also for their therapy. "I don't know how I am messing them up, but I know I am. The least I can do is help them pay for professional help!" she joked.

The decisions that mothers make—from the eating habits they teach their kids to how they respond to misbehavior and how they communicate love—greatly affect their children. As moms, we know this. Our past only confirms this fact. It doesn't

"He was twenty-nine, living in L.A. I came across this big musty box of baseball cards just cluttering up the house, so I tossed them. Today, they'd be worth $80,000."

Reprinted by permission of John McPherson, as appeared in Chicken Soup for the Soul Cartoons for Moms.

take much reflection to conjure up realities of how your mother's strengths and weaknesses have affected you. Many among us continue to deal with scars from our own mothers' failures. This makes us acutely aware and fearful of how our imperfections may be magnified in the lives of our children.

Both deliberate and incidental mistakes that mothers make have the potential to substantially alter the course of their children's lives. I recently met with a young mother who was feeding her child on her lap at a restaurant. Along with the food, the mother ordered coffee. While arranging the food on the table, the toddler pulled the coffee off the table onto his lap. The hot liquid absorbed into his clothes causing third-degree burns. The boy required several months of hospitalization and surgery to recover. Even so, he will bear the scars of this accident for the rest of his life.

Stories such as this drive fear into the hearts of mothers. It only takes one minute of lapse or one seemingly harmless decision to cause tragedy in the lives of our children. Accidents, mishaps, poor decisions and those seeking to harm our children seem to lurk in every corner, reminding us of how important it is that we be perfect. At countless times in my own parenting, a close call could have been a tragedy.

What about the little choices that we make every day? Isn't it the daily interactions that result in the values and decisions our children ultimately choose? The mother of a pregnant fifteen-year-old searches memories of her daughter's childhood to discover what misleading messages she may have given or mistakes she made that have led to this misfortune. A teenage son is kicked out of school for involvement with drugs. How might parenting failures have contributed to these mistakes?

> The combination of a mother's influence and her imperfections create guilt.

The combination of a mother's influence and her imperfections create guilt. Every mother knows that she will fail to influence her children perfectly. She will, therefore, wonder if weaknesses or struggles in her child's life are the result of her failure.

WHY WE FEEL GUILTY

Although guilt is no stranger to the average mother, we usually do not think about our guilt and understand its significance in our lives. Like a pesky bee that buzzes and threatens to sting at any time, we try to swat away guilt or dodge its path. Rarely do we tackle it head on.

Feelings of guilt result when you believe that you have failed at something. When you do something "wrong," your own sense of justice tells you that you deserve punishment. Even if no one else is aware of your shortcomings, you may actually develop ways of punishing yourself, like feeling depressed, repeating self-condemning statements, isolating, avoiding pleasurable activities or overindulging in them. Causing yourself to *feel* the uncomfortable angst of guilt is often the way you atone for imperfections. *If I beat myself up emotionally for a few hours, I will have paid for my mistake,* you may subconsciously reason.

Although feeling guilty should result from actually being guilty, the two often are incongruent. Some mothers experience false guilt, feeling guilty for things that are completely out of their control, while other mothers feel no guilt when their choices have done great harm to their children. While one mother is tormented over leaving her three-year-old son with his grandmother for a weekend, another mother feels no guilt about taking drugs and drinking throughout her entire pregnancy.

As most of us fall somewhere in the middle, how does guilt relate to the average day of a mother? She wakes up late and the whole family is rushing around to get ready for school. She throws together breakfast, packs lunches and is in a frantic search to find a lost shoe. The morning is chaotic, and she has not uttered a single kind word to her loved ones. Her words are filled with demands and reprimands. Her children easily pick up on her frustration and irritation. The buzz around the kitchen is "Don't mess with Mom. She's in a bad mood!" The school bus finally pulls away, and Mom is left to pick up the messes of the morning, the one in the kitchen and the one in her mind. She begins to berate herself for her behavior. *Why was I such a grump today? I felt totally out of control of my emotions. Why can't I just be more loving? More organized?*

When we evaluate our own sense of guilt, it is important to come to grips with what crimes we have actually committed to deserve the sentence of "guilty." Take the hassled mom in the above paragraph. What did she really do wrong? Yes, she was disorganized. She also was irritable with her family and did not give them a warm send-off for the day. These are her "crimes." Does she deserve punishment? You and I would acknowledge these as normal experiences of motherhood. Every woman has days when she feels harried and is less than affectionate with her children and husband. If this were my friend sitting across the table, confessing her morning failure, I would reassure her and encourage her to cut herself some slack. Wouldn't you? However, when it comes to my own mothering, dealing with normal imperfections often causes nagging feelings of guilt that are not so easily rationalized away.

We Feel Guilty Because We Sin

Confronting the problem of guilty feelings requires each of us to ask, *Am I truly guilty? Have I failed?* At the basic level, the answer is yes. All of us are guilty of sin. The Bible says that we were conceived in sin and, like all humanity, have an innate tendency to rebel against God. Adam and Eve experienced the first pangs of guilt as they hid from God after realizing their sinful choices. They tried casting blame, but their reality of guilt was inescapable. The verdict of "guilty" has since been rendered to "Adam's fallen race." Yes, there are times as mothers that we fail because of our sin. We can be short-tempered, selfish, deceitful, stubborn, unkind and manipulative. *That is the fact of our guilt.*

Unrelenting feelings of unworthiness and guilt sometimes result from sin that has never been addressed. Meredith came for counseling complaining of a vague sense of unhappiness in her life. She was a single mom of one son, Scott, who was born out of wedlock. As a successful businesswoman, Meredith could provide well for her son and could afford many of the luxuries that are supposed to bring happiness. She lavished Scott with gifts, vacations, the finest clothes and toys. Any time she sensed Scott was unhappy, she desperately tried to fix the problem but always seemed to come up empty. When he was cut from the baseball team, or when he struggled with algebra, his explosive adolescent temper—all reminded her of how inadequate she was as a mom. As Meredith talked about her motherhood experience, the tears began to flow. "I feel so guilty that I can't give him a dad and brothers and sisters! Nothing will ever be enough to make up for bringing him into this world without a real family!" Although Meredith was troubled by a thousand things that made her feel inadequate, the primary source of her guilt was an action that had occurred many years before.

When we sin against God, guilty feelings are healthy. They make us aware of our need for forgiveness. We feel convicted because we *are* guilty. People who ignore their sin will never experience the need to restore their relationship with God. This is the very reason that Jesus gave His life on the cross. He has paid for our sin, our deliberate rebellion and our inherent sinful nature.

In his excellent book *No Condemnation,* psychologist Dr. Bruce Narramore distinguishes between guilt that causes depression and "godly sorrow" that makes us aware of our need for repentance and dependence upon the Savior. While godly sorrow awakens our drive for maturity, guilt only serves to drive home the lie of our worthlessness. Godly sorrow energizes, but guilt paralyzes.

> Our guilty feelings are good when they cause us to repent from sin and accept Christ's sacrifice for our offenses.

Healthy guilt brings us face-to-face with our sin. There are only two responses we can have to our awareness of our guilt: Seek God's forgiveness through complete dependence on Christ, or try to make things right on our own. Only the first can free us from the bondage of guilt. Trying to be perfect or compensating for our mistakes is like running on a constant treadmill that squanders our energy and focus. Our guilty feelings are good when they cause us to repent from sin and accept Christ's sacrifice for our offenses.

We Feel Guilty Because We Are Imperfect

Although sin plays a major part in a mother's guilt, most of the moms that I have counseled are more paralyzed by guilt resulting from imperfections than from sin.

- ♡ A mother of a thirteen-year-old girl learns that her daughter was molested by a trusted relative. "I should have known. I should have protected her!"
- ♡ After years of nagging, scolding and punishing her son for inferior schoolwork, a mother learns that her son is

dyslexic. "All this time I thought he wasn't trying hard enough. I feel so guilty for all of those years I disciplined him when he was doing the best he could."

Forgetfulness, naiveté and inadequacy are not sins, although they may result in parenting mistakes. Sometimes a mother can be giving her best effort to love her children and still end up with a guilt-inducing mess.

Almost thirty years later, my mother still feels pangs of guilt for what our family refers to as "the Easter massacre." Mom loves holidays and always went overboard to make them special for us. One Easter morning, Mom woke us up by saying, "I have a big surprise for you kids in the basement."

The six of us ran downstairs to see what delight Mom had waiting for us. Soon, the bloodcurdling screams of terrified children were heard throughout the house. Mom had bought six live baby bunnies for us and hid them in a box in the basement. What my mom did not realize is that during the night the German shepherd thought the bunnies were his Easter present!

Being imperfect is no sin, but our mistakes can potentially harm our children. How can you take away the "guilt" of a mother who had to be away from her children for months because of a medical condition? Or a mother whose husband walked out on the family to be with another woman? Or a mother who passed on a genetic illness to her child? Or a mother who is so depressed that she can barely force herself to get out of bed?

Whether you are battling guilt from extreme circumstances or you feel guilty for putting your child in the church nursery, unhealthy guilt can rob you of your joy and focus as a mother. How are you to respond to the daily mistakes and sinful choices you make in normal life? Are the resulting guilty feelings your friend or foe?

What Role Does Guilt Have in Parenting?

Feeling bad about our mistakes can be a strong motivator for change. If the cranky mother described earlier never felt guilty about her attitude and behavior, she would likely repeat it daily. You can be sure that my mom was more careful about where she hid bunnies on future Easters! Although normal imperfection is a natural part of motherhood, isn't there also a place to strive for maturity and growth? When we feel the most inadequate as mothers is often when we gain the motivation to seek the wisdom and direction to become more adequate. In fact, you probably picked up this book because of your awareness of parenting mistakes you have made (or at least fear making).

Even though we are under the blood of Christ, we still strive for His righteousness. The Bible says that our sins are "remembered no more" once we confess them and place our trust in Christ for forgiveness (Heb. 8:12). However, our mistakes still grieve us. Most sobering is the fact that our sins and mistakes still have consequences.

Consider David's sins of adultery and murder. He was tortured by his guilt before he fully confessed his sin before God. God forgave him and lifted the guilty sentence from him. However, God expected David to clean up his act and also did not remove many of the consequences of David's sin

> God has not intended His children to parent in a spirit of fear. There is a difference between diligently seeking to be a godly parent and cowering from guilt of the past and fear of the future.

from his family. Imagine David's sorrow when his son Amnon raped his daughter Tamar. It increased when another son, Absalom, killed Amnon in revenge. David had to know that this was the fulfillment of the promise of 1 Samuel 12 that the sword would never leave his family as the result of his own sin.

Our sins and oversights, whether or not they are intentional, have a detrimental impact on our children. We make mistakes and we wrestle with the potential consequences of those mistakes. However, God has not intended His children to parent in a spirit of fear. There is a difference between diligently seeking to be a godly parent and cowering from guilt of the past and fear of the future.

Although feelings of guilt and inadequacy can be motivators to seek what we lack, they also can be incapacitating. For many mothers, their self-condemning thoughts and doubts only add to their real inadequacies rather than encourage growth.

For Sarah, a mother of four children, this pattern of behavior was certainly the case. She was very aware of her many inadequacies as a mother. She was so easily overwhelmed by the demands and needs of her children that she found herself reacting irritably and angrily as a rule rather than as the exception. She wanted to be loving and giving toward her children, but she rarely had the composure and patience to do so while with them. Almost daily she regretted her harshly spoken words and her explosive temper. When feeling particularly guilty, she would let them stay up late, eat junk food for dinner and generally give into their demands. As a result of her permissiveness, Sarah's children became more difficult to manage. The cycle of her inadequacy, guilt and overcompensation continued.

In many ways our bondage to guilt makes us less prepared to parent rather than encouraging maturity. While some, like Sarah, overcompensate with lavishness, other mothers overreact with structure and lists that provide tangible reassurance that they are doing something according to plan. Still others sink into depression and despair, sapping their energy and enthusiasm for parenting. Mothers of teenage and adult children may begin to project their guilty feelings onto their children. The message they communicate is: "It's not that I am an imperfect mother. You are an imperfect and ungrateful child. It's your fault." Many adult children still deal with mothers who have become masters of manipulating and pouring guilt onto their children to avoid acknowledging their own failures in parenting.

So, how does a sinful, imperfect mother navigate through the overwhelming job of parenting without damaging her children and paying daily homage to the altar of maternal guilt? Can't God see the heart of a woman who desperately wants to be a great mom for her children? Won't He bless her tireless efforts even if they are flawed?

Guilt-free parenting is only possible when we move from a worldly perspective to a godly perspective.

The parenting prescription of the world places people in the position of gods. Parents create children, define their morality, manipulate their children's lives and therefore must take full responsibility for the end result. The world screams its own "wisdom" at moms, telling them to do more, to be more and to worry more. The ultimate goal of motherhood is to design a happy and productive person.

The world has its own deluge of standards to determine whether you are succeeding or failing as a mom. In fact, society may judge you to be a roaring success one day and a dismal failure the next. And you'd better get it right, because your children's lives are all riding on your shoulders!

In buying into this thinking, we parent believing that we must be perfect (or nearly so) to raise perfect (or nearly perfect) children. We base our performance on how our children are presently behaving. We believe that good mothers, without exception, are those who produce good children. We look to a host of indicators throughout the job of motherhood to determine whether or not we are actually accomplished parents.

In stark contrast, godly wisdom begins with fearing God, acknowledging that He alone is the author of life—ours and our children's. He has placed our children in our homes for His purpose and plan. He has given us very specific instructions in His Word about what we should teach our young children and how to model His love. His own example as our Father demonstrates for us how to respect and respond to the budding free will of an adolescent. Ultimately, His power and sovereignty remind us that motherhood is a servant's call, not to our children but to our Savior. We parent not out of possessiveness or personal needs, but out of devotion to God and faithfulness to His Word.

Although good parenting does usually result in good children, God wants us to be more invested in the *process* of raising our kids rather than in the outcome. He has not called us to raise perfect children, but *to be faithful with the influence He has given us. Above all, He wants us to depend upon His wisdom and entrust our children into His care as we seek as mothers to glorify Him.*

After all, whom are we really serving in this journey called motherhood? Why do we make all of the sacrifices (lack of sleep, loss of figure, loss of sanity . . . must I go on?)? Why are we so desperate to succeed as mothers? Parenting, even in a secular home, is such a noble endeavor that we often are unaware of how misguided our efforts can be. Because we give our time and energy to our kids, we assume that we are serving God through our motherhood. I know that far too often, my motivation as a mother is entrenched in my all-consuming love for my kids and my compulsive drive to parent "right." The actions look great, but my heart is invested in a very subtle form of idolatry. Do I really want to please God through motherhood, or am I committed to my own agenda?

Forty-eight-year-old Tricia was the mother of three children. Kate, her oldest, was married and expecting twins. Al, nineteen, was serving overseas in the Army. Tim, sixteen, was a sophomore in high school. Like any mom, Tricia had doubts and worries regarding her kids. She also had her share of critics. Then, the unthinkable happened—she was diagnosed with terminal cancer.

Tricia sought counseling not only to prepare her children for the coming loss, but to address the question, "Did I do a good enough job?" She would never see the end result of her motherhood, but she wanted the peace of knowing that she had pleased God throughout her life. As she shared her fears and sadness of leaving her husband and children, her words were profound. "At first I was so angry that God would take me before my job of parenting was done. I thought about everything that I will be missing: grandchildren I would never meet, weddings I wouldn't attend, wounds that I couldn't comfort and choices that I couldn't influence. It tore me apart. Then I realized that God has allowed me to finish my race. My goal as a mother used to be to raise my kids to be wonderful adults. I am beginning to understand that my job is simply to honor God through each day that I have. Once I accepted this, it was so comforting to not have to be responsible for what I can't control!"

Guilt-free motherhood is possible when we choose to serve and glorify God through our efforts as moms. Like Tricia, we need a drastic shift in our thinking. Instead of feeling fully responsible for the lives of our children, we become fully responsible for our faithfulness to our Savior. We let go of burdens that we were never meant to carry. We become servants of His plan, not architects of our own.

Throughout this book, we will search together for God's blueprint for motherhood: godly wisdom. My prayer is that this is a powerful resource in your journey to discovering a maternity free of the shadow and bondage of guilt. I pray that the words on each page provide a tool to equip you in the awesome ministry of motherhood.

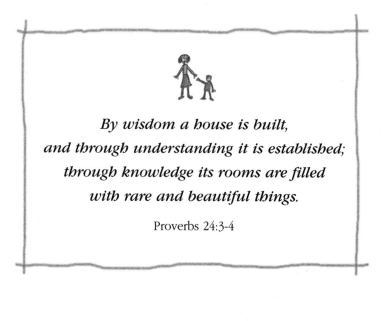

By wisdom a house is built,
and through understanding it is established;
through knowledge its rooms are filled
with rare and beautiful things.

Proverbs 24:3-4

For Personal Reflection

1. What are some things that you have felt or feel guilty about as a mother?

_____

_____

2. When you "fail" as a mom, does the resulting guilt you feel draw you closer to dependence upon God or push you away from Him?

_____

_____

3. Do ever feel like you have to be perfect as a mom? If so, how does this impact your parenting?

_____

_____

2

Hey, Lady! You're Leaking Influence!

Not long ago, I started out the week with about one hundred dollars in cash in my wallet. Because my husband and I try not to have much cash on hand, this was a treat for me. Little things that I normally passed by now became enticing. During the week, I visited Starbucks a few times for overpriced coffee. I also took my kids out for lunch instead of making food at home. I had the car washed and picked up a few odds and ends at the mall. By the time Friday rolled around, my wallet was empty. When Mike and I talked about going to see a movie, he asked me if I had any spending cash we could use for our date. I was a little embarrassed to admit that all of the cash was gone. "What did you spend it on?" he asked. As I thought about it, I realized that I had spent the money haphazardly—a little here, a little there—and it had disappeared. We ended up renting a movie and warming up some pizza from the freezer. That money could have funded a romantic date, but without much thought, I had squandered it.

The way we spend cash is often similar to the manner in which we use our influence as parents. No doubt, God has given us great resources to guide our children. Every day, we wake up with hours on the clock to spend. We exchange words with our kids that affect them throughout the day. We have chances to teach, discipline, guide and love. What's more, God has a specific purpose for which we are to use that influence. Unfortunately, like loose cash, we often end up spending our influence on things that are relatively meaningless to the task of parenting.

Instead of parenting based on godly wisdom, we often approach motherhood by reacting to the continuous pulls both in our environment and within ourselves. Our emotions and fears, our children's demands, societal expectations and the opinions of others are strong forces that compel us to react to them. Without definitive direction, we react to whatever internal or external pressures bode well in the moment. A neighbor declares that you are too strict with your children. All of a sudden, you begin doubting your discipline. Your son starts giving you the silent treatment after you enforced a curfew. Is it really worth risking your relationship with him?

Nothing is more likely to fuel the guilt cycle of a mother than reactive parenting. Ironically, reactive parenting feeds guilt while at the same time promising to alleviate it. The more you doubt your parenting, the more you make decisions reactively. As you evaluate the haphazard way you parent, your feelings of inadequacy escalate.

If you were the president of the United States, how would you know whether or not you were doing a good job? On any given day, you could find both staunch supporters and angry critics. On the same issue, people would both praise you and despise you. Certainly the poll of public opinion would be an erratic guidepost. Should you look at economic indices like unemployment and the national deficit to determine a job well done? Or might you judge your success on the state of America's international relationships? What about the predominant moral direction of the country?

A president could frantically pursue all of these indicators of accomplishment. But while chasing success in this manner, he would inherently become ineffective. His time, energy and focus would be misspent pleasing the crowd and trying to influence factors beyond his control. His decision making would be driven by superficial guideposts rather than by conviction and wise counsel. Could he be a great president even if much of the country disliked him? Could he be successful even if the economy was poor or foreign relations were strained?

Although the image of sitting behind a desk in the Oval Office is far-fetched, the dilemma is very close to home. How do you know if you are a good mother? What indicators do you chase, hoping to prove yourself successful? What editorials, household meters and polls of popular opinion do you check regularly to assuage your anxiety? Like money spent rather thoughtlessly, much of our influence in our job of parenting may seem to have been spent chasing shallow assurances of successful motherhood.

This chapter examines a few of the many pressures that lure us into reactive parenting. Each is a superficial barometer that answers the question, "Am I a good mother?" While these external definitions of our success appear to be gauges that allay our fear of inadequacy, they often end up contributing to it. Although they may provide temporary sanctuary from feelings of doubt and insecurity, the end result is the precious influence of a mother squandered.

REACTING TO THE DEMANDS OF YOUR CHILDREN

"I took Joey to a Yankees game last week for his birthday. He loves the Yankees, and I thought it would be a really special surprise. The whole night, he sat in his seat with a glum look on his face. I couldn't get him to say a word. I even bought him a Derek Jeter jersey. I don't know what it will take to make him happy these days. No matter what I do, I can't seem to be a good enough mother for him. In fact, it seems like he'd rather not have me around at all."

When your children are affectionate, loving and happy, you usually feel like a good mom. When they can't stand to be in the same room as you or cringe at the sound of your voice, you probably feel like a pretty lousy mom. A happy, contented child is surely a sign that you are a good mother, isn't it? If so, then do whatever you can to keep those kiddos smiling!

I think we underestimate how much of our influence is spent reacting to the demands and displeasure of our kids.

> Without realizing it, we make many decisions based on our children's momentary happiness.

We place a great deal of weight on whether or not our kids are pleased with how we are parenting. Without realizing it, we make many decisions based on our children's momentary happiness. Sometimes, we want to please them. Other times, we frankly just want peace and quiet.

"Mom, I'm starving. I need a snack," one child whines.

"Dinner will be ready in half an hour. You can wait."

"No, I can't," the child retorts. "I am so hungry I can't stand it."

After three such requests, Mom replies in frustration, "Would you leave me alone? Go play with your brother while I finish making dinner!"

"I don't want to play. I want to watch TV."

"No," the mom insists. "Go keep yourself busy, for goodness sake!"

The little boy stomps out of the kitchen to find something to keep him busy. Within five minutes the boys are fighting. Into the kitchen they run, screaming at each other. Mom is on the phone, the pasta is boiling over and the rolls are burning in the oven. At this point, she is likely to do anything to buy peace. Soon, both children are sitting quietly in the living room eating chips and watching cartoons.

What mother hasn't felt the exasperation that causes her to give in to her child's demands—whether it's the toy he's been begging for nonstop all week, the party she has asked to go to eight times in the last half an hour or the vegetables he stubbornly insists on not eating? The simple truth is that children are often much more committed to the agenda of getting what they want than their parents are to parenting wisely. The average kid has much more time and energy to devote to lobbying than his mother does to staying consistent.

"Ummm . . . just a minute, Mom!"

Reprinted by permission of John McPherson, as appeared in Chicken Soup for the Soul Cartoons for Moms.

As moms, we seem most vulnerable to giving in to our children's demands when we are desperate for their behavior to change. A child screaming in the grocery store is almost assured of receiving something to please or pacify her. "If you stop crying, I'll buy you some candy." Mom is in crisis-management mode and will do almost anything to stop drawing the attention of the entire store to her child. The teenager who is threatening involvement in drugs or sex may have tremendous leverage with his parents if he promises to clean up his act.

A child's bad behavior makes parents feel desperate with their influence. Bargaining becomes a dangerous tool that savvy children exploit to get their own way. To temporarily make the danger, discomfort or fear go away, parents often sell the ranch. By appeasing their children, they have calmed the storm but have set the precedent for letting their children determine how parental influence is used.

All of us have given in to our children's demands when we know we shouldn't have, which does not make us bad parents. However, we need to determine whether we have adopted the *pattern* of using our influence based on the demands of our children. Unfortunately, our society as a whole has adopted a philosophy that caters to children's demands. A trip to the mall or listening to the casual conversation of children proves the predominant theme of parents constantly catering to their children's desires and whims. Sadly, we live in a culture of spoiled children who have not learned character traits like self-discipline, delayed gratification, gratefulness and kindness to others. This epidemic has resulted from the predominant cultural belief that good parents produce happy children. What a breath of fresh air it is to come across parents who value character more than momentary bliss in their homes!

Recently some friends of ours took their children to an amusement park a few hours from home. From the beginning, their eight-year-old daughter had a very demanding attitude about the day. She whined about what they had for lunch and complained that the family did not immediately go on the attractions she wanted to ride first. Our friends warned their daughter several times that her attitude needed to change—that she should be grateful for the opportunity to have such an outing. Her ingratitude and selfishness continued for about an hour. At that point, the mother took the daughter out of the park and sat with her in the car for approximately two hours while the father and other children enjoyed the day. Late in the afternoon, the daughter reentered the park with a dramatically different attitude.

This family tolerated some relatively minor inconvenience to teach their daughter a very valuable lesson. Rather than give in to her demands, they showed the young girl that her selfishness would not be rewarded. Although this approach sounds like a very commonsense way to parent, in the moment, most adults would not have the discipline and commitment to take such a step. After all, the tickets to get into the park were almost fifty dollars each; they had driven several hours and had looked forward to this outing for weeks. What mom wants to sit in a hot parking lot with her pouting child just as a matter of principle? But wouldn't you gladly pay one hundred dollars and be uncomfortable for a few hours to teach your child the lifelong lesson of gratefulness?

Parenting is often an unpopular job. Parenting well will mean that our kids sometimes loathe us and that we may have to make some inconvenient and politically incorrect decisions. Reacting to their desires and demands is so much easier in the short run. But basing your success as a mother on the relative happiness of your children is like chasing the wind.

REACTING TO THE EXPECTATIONS OF OTHERS

"Every time I am at my parents' house I feel like a terrible mother. Whenever my kids misbehave, I can just sense my mom's disapproving look. She thinks I don't push Bryan hard enough in school and that I baby Samantha. She, of all people, should know how difficult parenting is!"

I sometimes wonder what it must feel like to be involved in a public profession like acting or professional athletics. Every morning, newspapers and media shows are devoted to analyzing the lives and decisions of people who are in the public eye. Most people who enjoy watching professional sports have an opinion about the call a coach made that decided the game, or the dropped pass that cost the team the playoffs. People who know very little about what it takes to be a professional athlete often make very harsh judgments and act like experts about "what should have been done."

Most of us as moms get a taste of this "parenting paparazzi" too. Think of how many people have opinions about how you parent. Friends, parents, siblings, aunts and uncles all often feel free to offer you advice on the mistakes they see you making. One thinks you are too strict while someone else encourages you to buckle down. If you are into pleasing the crowd, good luck! Someone always disagrees with your methods.

Like it or not, the opinions of others often have a tremendous impact on how we parent. Raising children is a long and arduous task. There are months and years in which the results of our efforts are far from obvious. We wonder, *Am I doing a good job? Will my kids turn out to be upstanding citizens?* Only time will tell, and time often takes longer to give the verdict than we would like. In the absence of solid evidence that we are parenting well, the opinions of others often become overly important.

> In the absence of solid evidence that we are parenting well, the opinions of others often become overly important.

Many of the interventions we use as parents take time, sometimes years, to have an effect. If the basis of our decisions is rooted in biblical wisdom, we can rely on our faith rather than taking a Gallup poll to assuage our insecurity. Certainly it is wise to seek counsel and ask for the input of trusted advisors. In fact, Proverbs 20:18 admonishes us to "Make plans by seeking advice." However, *much of the input we listen to is based on a compulsive need to reassure our fears rather than a sincere quest for wisdom.* Solicited and not, often advice can be just as likely to be wrong as right. Many parents have felt assured in making poor decisions because someone in their lives approved. In the same manner, many parents bear the brunt of years of criticism only to have time prove that their parenting methods were appropriate. Even well-meaning input can be far off-base.

We naturally want others to view us as good mothers. Our parenting seems to take place under the microscope of others who make judgments as they watch us interact with our children. This unspoken pressure can dramatically influence our parenting.

One day, after I had finished teaching a seminar on parenting, I took my children to lunch. A lady approached our table to tell me how much she enjoyed my presentation. I thanked her for her encouragement and introduced my kids. Somewhere in the deep recesses of my children's brains must be a signal that says "This would be a great time to test Mom." Perhaps it was just God keeping me humble. For whatever reason, the kids took the opportunity to demonstrate to this lady that Mom still has some things to learn about parenting. They whined, complained and argued with each other throughout the entire lunch. Nothing I did seemed to have the desired effect of bringing out their more angelic side. Talk about feeling inadequate under the spotlight!

In retrospect, I am a normal mom. I have normal kids. At times they misbehave, and I make mistakes. How short-sighted for me to put additional pressure on them, or on my parenting, because I am supposed to be an "expert"! If I parent based on the need to appear perfect to others, I am sure to fail. Doing so would mean that I have devoted my influence to pleasing the crowd rather than to raising my children according to God's calling. At the end of the day, what someone thinks of my mothering is inconsequential, but it sure feels important in the moment. Parenting, like every task we attempt, must be done with the focus of pleasing God, not man (Col. 3:23, Gal. 1:10).

REACTING TO THE PRESSURES AND BUSINESS OF THE DAY

"Life is so hectic right now, but I am afraid if I slow down I will miss something. Homework, sports teams, sleepovers, youth group, music lessons. I feel so much pressure to keep up with it all."

The life of a mother is so full—full of fun, love and happiness. But it is also full of worry, frustration and endless demands. There is no time to be reflective or even relaxed. Motherhood sometimes feels like a blur. We find ourselves totally unprepared for the next challenge or stage of our children's lives because we are still trying to catch up with yesterday's worries and messes. There is perhaps no greater cause of reactive parenting than the demands of the day.

"Mom, will you play with me? Will you read me a book? Will you help me with my homework?" How often do I answer these questions with, "No, honey, I can't. I've got to . . . go to the mall, return some phone calls, clean the house, do the laundry, get dinner started, check e-mail, change a diaper, water the garden."

Reprinted by permission of John McPherson, as appeared in Chicken Soup for the Soul Cartoons for Moms.

Of course, these things have to be done. Exclusively doting on my children all day would be neither realistic nor healthy. But it can seem like days and weeks that I am short-tempered and emotionally unavailable because of all of the things that have to be done.

Not being busy enough is cause for many women to feel guilty. "How will my four-year-old learn social skills if she is not in play group?" "My daughter won't develop her musical potential if we don't enroll her in music lessons." "We really should be more involved in church." "Why can't I juggle life as well as Heather?"

American culture is filled with opportunities for wonderful activities for our children. Birthday parties, church socials, sports teams, gymnastics, choir, scouting. Keeping kids busy in productive activities is important. But where is the balance?

After a couple years of driving their three children to every event under the sun, Kim and Eric decided to scale back. Each of their children was allowed to choose one sport per year to participate in. Outside of Wednesday night youth group, they also curtailed all involvement during weeknights so the kids could focus on schoolwork and family time. Each month they said "no" to a dozen wonderful activities. At times, the kids complained that they were missing out. Other times, Eric and Kim felt peer pressure from other parents.

Our society promotes activity and busyness as a primary indicator of success in parenting. Our busyness is often an effort to avoid feeling guilty. The hard work of parenting is often done in the quiet of home, through countless conversations and hours of prayer. Reacting to the demands of busyness invariably distracts us from God's purpose for us as parents. Someone once said, "Failure can be succeeding at something that really doesn't matter."

REACTING TO YOUR EMOTIONS

"I don't even like Jacob anymore. I feel terrible saying this, but I dread when he walks through the door in the afternoon. What kind of mother can't stand her son?"

Throughout my life, I have never felt stronger emotions than the ones evoked by my children. Usually not one to show much sentiment, I was completely out of control of my emotions the moment I met each of our children. All I could do was weep. While my husband commented on our sons' features and discussed information the doctor was sharing, I felt like a blubbering idiot. Even now, all I have to do is let my mind wander to the memories of my children's births to feel the majesty of the moment. Likewise, imagining one of them hurt or killed can instantly bring waves of panic, fear and grief. Every now and then I find myself becoming vehemently aggressive with someone who has threatened or hurt my children in even the slightest way. Motherhood has brought me face-to-face with feelings I never knew I had.

Less noble than the emotions stemming from my maternal love is the anger that one of my dear, sweet little ones can stir in me. I had always considered myself a patient person, until I had children. Then came the question that has been asked for the fiftieth time, the kids fighting while I am trying to get through rush-hour traffic, the clothes that still lay on the floor after ten reminders to tidy up, discovering that my four-year-old decorated the bathroom with my lipstick, or the dinners that go uneaten because "I don't like that!" They all have a way of short-cutting my long-suffering nature and getting right to my anger. Ten years ago, I never would have believed it if I saw a movie of me losing it with my kids. Over the silliest things, my mild manner can suddenly transform into a cross between the Incredible Hulk and the Wicked Witch of the West.

Sadness, fear, depression, anger, joy and guilt are all emotions we undoubtedly feel strongly as mothers. Unfortunately, these feelings have the ability to override our logic and best intentions and dominate our behavior and decisions. For the same offense, you may treat your child drastically different based on your current emotional state. One day, you are nurturing; the next you have trouble keeping yourself from screaming. We have all been there.

Responding emotionally is a tremendous cause of guilt for the average mother. Yelling, playing favorites, overprotectiveness and inconsistent discipline are all ways of parenting reactively to strong emotions. Looking back on reactive parenting causes moms to feel guilty about being so irrational.

Certainly, emotions are not all bad. A mother void of emotions would likely be stoic and insensitive to her child's needs.

Part of the uniqueness that a mother offers her child is her ability to form an emotional connection. Her emotions can be valuable indicators and prompts to alter parenting based on the subtleties of a child's emotional needs. However, emotions can also override all logic, creating erratic, unpredictable and chaotic parenting. Emotions can be effective guides, but they can also be deceptive distractions. Although strong feelings may help fine-tune parenting, they are not good guideposts for establishing consistent parenting principles.

Over the past few months, twelve-year-old Steven has been quite a challenge for his mother, Andrea. Usually an easygoing kid, Steven now mopes around the house, snaps at his siblings, complains about completing chores and talks back to his mom. Andrea is angry at him most of the time and misses the affectionate child he once was. She is frustrated at her inability to get him out of his pre-adolescent funk.

Andrea is often tempted to react impulsively to her emotions. While sometimes she wants to scream at Steven out of anger, other times she feels like begging him to be kind. More than once she has felt frustrated enough to melt into tears. Although none of these emotional reactions would promote effective parenting, each of Andrea's feelings is an important component of responding to Steven's behavior. Her anger alerts her to his disrespect and need for correction. Her sadness prompts her to prepare for the inevitable changes in their relationship as Steven enters adolescence. Her frustration reminds her to seek both help and support through this stage of motherhood.

Good parenting is achieved when your emotions *inform* your decisions. Both your own feelings and those of your children are valuable pieces of information that aid in acting effectively. Poor parenting results when emotions override the larger goals of parenting and become the major impetus behind your reactions to your children. Can you discern when your feelings help your parenting and when you become too emotionally reactive to your children?

> Good parenting is achieved when your emotions *inform* your decisions. Poor parenting results when emotions override the larger goals of parenting.

REACTING TO YOUR CHILDHOOD

"I don't care if I am not a perfect mom as long as my child doesn't have to suffer through what I did. As long as I do a better job than my parents did, I can be happy with my parenting."

For many parents, there is no more revealing moment than when they find themselves repeating patterns that they swore they would change from their own childhood. "I can't believe it. I sound just like my mother!"

Even those with largely positive childhood experiences can think of a few things that they are determined not to repeat as they parent their own children. As young adults, they evaluated their parents' mistakes and made vows to themselves like, *I will never make my children wear ragged hand-me-downs,* or *I'm never going to be overprotective like my mom was with me. Kids need to live and learn from their mistakes.*

The way each of us was parented drastically affects the manner in which we evaluate our own parenting. Some people are happy to repeat the largely healthy interactions that took place in their childhood home. For others, memories of discord and dysfunction create a tremendous fear of passing their demons on to the next generation. Sexual abuse, alcohol or drug addiction, mental illness, domestic violence, divorce, neglect, abandonment, unreasonable expectations and humiliation each plant permanent messages and fears within the children who have witnessed them. The process or even the prospect of parenting can dramatically resurrect strong emotions and memories from one's childhood.

The past can lead to reactive parenting in two ways. First, many parents unwittingly repeat the past with their own children. From the dramatic cycle of abusive relationships to more subtle patterns like a dominating mother, people commonly yet unconsciously replay their own childhood dynamics as they parent. Some people explain this phenomenon as generational sin as Scripture suggests—others delve into complicated psychological reasons. No doubt, both explanations are true reflections of what occurs in many homes.

Many biblical stories provide excellent examples of repeated generational patterns. Abraham and Sarah doubted that God would send them the child He had promised them. So, Abraham had a child with Hagar, Sarah's maid. The boy's name was Ishmael. Eventually, Sarah conceived the promised child, Isaac. There was tremendous sibling rivalry between the two boys. Eventually, Ishmael and his mother were kicked out of the home. Isaac and his wife Rebekah, had twins, Jacob and Esau. The pattern of favoritism and fraternal strife continued between the twins. Isaac loved Esau and Rebekah loved Jacob. With his mother's help, Jacob conned his brother out of his blessing and birthright. He then had twelve sons with three different wives. He openly favored Joseph, lavishing him with expensive gifts. His brothers were so angry with Joseph that they attempted to murder him and then sold him into slavery. With each generation, the favoritism became more blatant and more destructive.

No one consciously sets out to repeat destructive family patterns. It usually happens when a person fails to evaluate and recognize harmful experiences from his or her own childhood. A person spends the first two decades of life learning how to interact with others. The negative as well as the positive lessons are firmly rooted in her understanding of relationships. How can someone change all she has learned without consciously determining to do so?

The second way the past can be detrimental to parenting is through overreaction. Some people are very aware of the scars of their own childhood. They staunchly determine that they will never repeat the destruction and pain they experienced as children. In an effort to do so, they may overcompensate, creating different problems in their own parenting.

For example, Sue grew up in a very chaotic home environment. Her father was practically never around. He traveled extensively and was regularly involved with other women. When he was home, Sue's father was short-tempered and cruel to the children. Sue's mother did her best to keep the family afloat, but the task emotionally overwhelmed her. By the time Sue reached adolescence, her mother had all but given up. Plagued with depression, her mother turned to alcohol. Sue, as the oldest of five children, assumed the role of the adult in the family. She cooked, kept the house running and looked after her siblings. As soon as she reached eighteen, Sue moved far away from her family home and managed to work her way through college.

Sue married Brian while in her early twenties. The couple waited to have children for almost a decade, largely because of Sue's fears of repeating the misery of her childhood. When they did start a family, Sue worked tirelessly to avoid her fears of the chaotic family life she had experienced. Everything was ordered. She clung to rigid schedules of mealtime, bedtime and playtime. There were lists and charts everywhere, with no room for spontaneity, laughter or enjoyment. Sue had also systematically all but eliminated Brian from parenting. In her quest to avoid chaos, she secured complete control of the household. Although she loved her husband, she couldn't trust him. Her only significant memory of a father was one who abused and abandoned his children.

Sue's determination to avoid the pain of her childhood is both understandable and justified. However, the compulsive manner in which she addressed her fears drastically interfered with her ability to meet her children's needs. Without realizing that she was doing so, Sue devoted the majority of her influence to managing her own fear rather than doing the job of godly parenting.

Evaluating the past is an important step to not repeating it. However, becoming overwhelmed or obsessed by a fear of the past can be just as enslaving as repeating negative patterns.

MOVING FROM REACTIVE TO PROACTIVE MOTHERHOOD

Resisting the pull to parent reactively is incredibly difficult. All of the forces discussed in this chapter can be stubborn and potent magnets for our influence. Reactive motherhood is compelling because it provides a yardstick by which we can measure our mothering. How busy we stay, how happy our kids are, the approval of others, undoing the past . . . they all help us alleviate the fear that we are failing as mothers. They provide tangible ways of evaluating our success. Unfortunately, they are superficial measures of parenthood that distract us from God's design for our influence. Although it may feel good in the moment, reactive parenting creates the very anxiety and guilt it was meant to alleviate!

Proactive parenting is the exact opposite of reactive parenting. Proactive parents make decisions and interact based on a set of predetermined goals and values. Along the way they evaluate whether or not they are on track. Like referring to a road map, they have a definite idea of the direction, broadly and specifically, that their parenting is to achieve. As time goes by and situations change, they revise and adjust their course. Sure, there may be days, weeks and even months where they feel lost or off course with their children. But proactive parents eventually consult and reflect upon the overarching principles of their parenting.

Avoiding guilt, as a mother, relies upon using our parental influence with very clear direction and focus. If we truly understand God's calling for us as mothers and strive to the best of our abilities to fulfill that mandate, we have nothing to regret, regardless of the outcome of our parenting. We can have peace that we have run the race that God has set for us. No second-guessing—no wondering what could have been. God never calls us to raise perfect children. However, He does expect us to be conscious and faithful with our tremendous influence as mothers.

The antidote to squandering our influence reactively is setting a proactive course of motherhood. But upon what road map should we set our course? With what blueprint do we build our house? By what truth should we parent our children?

The following chapters lay out a blueprint for motherhood based on the truths found in God's Word and His creation. My words are human. However, my intention is to direct you to the well of truth and wisdom that God offers to His children.

*A discerning man keeps wisdom
in view, but a fool's eyes wander
to the ends of the earth.*

Proverbs 17:24

For Personal Reflection

1. What assurances do you chase after when you feel inadequate as a mother? _____

2. How does the busyness of motherhood keep you in a reactive mode with your kids? What important aspects of parenting are neglected because of your busyness? _____
   _____

3. How are you tempted to parent differently when others are watching?
   _____

4. How do your emotions impact your parenting? _____

5. What salient messages and patterns (both positive and negative) from your own childhood impact your parenting? In what ways do you tend to react to your past? _____
   _____

Part II

A Blueprint for Motherhood

The Forest for the Trees

As I write this, our third son, Christian, is just shy of two weeks old. I am in one of the worst physical times of motherhood. There are fluids flowing out of almost every opening of my body; I have hives, hemorrhoids, an incision across my lower abs, gas pains and sore nipples; and I have not slept more than two hours straight in over a month. The other day my husband commented on how tired he was, and I almost punched him. And don't even put me near a scale! Going to the bathroom feels like giving birth all over again. On top of that, my stomach looks like a crumpled paper bag, and the only clothes that fit me are sweatpants. I cry at the drop of a hat and generally feel like a fat, depressed, leaking zombie.

At a point like this, it's easy to question why I became a mother—for the third time! Am I just trying to raise happy, healthy kids so that they can get married and raise their happy, healthy kids? I know I share this periodic uncertainty with most mothers. We want all of our maternal sacrifice to result in something significant. However, that "something significant" is hard to define in the midst of motherhood.

"I'll give you a hundred bucks if you'll watch my kids for twenty minutes while I take a nap."

Reprinted by permission of John McPherson, as appeared in Chicken Soup for the Soul Cartoons for Moms.

My guess is that very, very few mothers have ever asked the question, "What does God intend for me to do with my influence as a mom?" Sure, all of us have cried out for help or direction when we have felt overwhelmed. But how many can say that they regularly seek godly direction in their perspective as parents? Well-meaning, dedicated moms are usually too busy keeping up with the demands of parenting to ever approach the task with a clear sense of calling or purpose.

Imagine hiring a team of builders to build your dream house. The building team arrives, and the foreman asks for the blueprint. You reply, "We don't have one. We were thinking we would just wing it as we go." As ridiculous as this sounds, most of us have used that approach for the task of building a family—a much more complicated and eternal task than building a home. Do you have a blueprint for your family?

If you have given your life to the Lord, the only way to begin preparing a blueprint for motherhood is to go to the Master Architect and seek His direction (Ps. 127:1). Our ultimate goal as mothers needs to be based on bringing glory to God. Consider these challenges from Paul's writings:

> So whether you eat or drink or whatever you do, do it all for the glory of God.
>
> (1 Cor. 10:31)

> And whatever you do, whether in word or deed, do it all in the name of the Lord Jesus, giving thanks to God the Father.
>
> (Col. 3:17)

Whatever you do, work at it with all your heart, as work-
ing for the Lord, not for men.

(Col. 3:23)

These verses define the bedrock of any Christian's endeavor. Certainly they apply to motherhood. Parenting is not separate from our church work, missions work or worship. It is an essential cornerstone of how we devote our lives to the Lord. As with anything else we put our hands to, a follower of Christ parents *all for the purpose of bringing glory to the Lord.* Without God's glory as our ultimate goal, we will someday have second thoughts and regrets. How can we avoid guilt unless we fulfill the purpose to which we have been called?

Although our motives may be on target, actually living them out can seem far more complicated. After all, how do we bring glory to God through making peanut butter sandwiches, saying bedtime prayers and sitting through piano recitals? How do we apply biblical teaching to the daily grind of motherhood?

WHERE THE RUBBER MEETS THE ROAD

As I strive to please God as a mom, I wrestle with the dilemma of translating the theoretical into the practical. Perhaps like you, my thoughts are filled with real concerns and uncertainties that often are not addressed in the Bible. Try finding chapter and verse for each of these common parenting questions:

♡ Is schedule or demand feeding better for my infant?

♡ What do I do when my one-year-old hits his brother?

♡ How should I deal with my daughter's temper tantrums?

♡ How do I know if my child is just fussy or if something is physically wrong?

♡ My child is almost four and still not potty-trained. What should I do?

♡ Should my child clean his plate or eat just what he wants?

♡ Why does my daughter whine so much?

♡ My son has a learning disability. How do I help him not feel stupid?

♡ My daughter is depressed. What do I do?

♡ How can I get my son to stop picking his nose?

♡ My husband and I are fighting a lot. How do I handle this with the kids?

♡ How do I teach my sixteen-year-old to be a responsible driver?

♡ My son is dating a girl I don't like. Do I tell him what I think?

Through responding to these questions and many more, we glorify God through the journey of motherhood. But how? The Bible doesn't tell us, does it?

The Bible rarely gives us precise answers to the questions we have as moms. No scriptural mandate tells you how to potty-train or what time your teenager's curfew should be. However,

God's Word does give us general and timeless principles that we can apply to the everyday life of motherhood. Embedded in Scripture is an effective *strategy* for addressing all the real-life questions we have. God has given each of us a practical key to unlocking the puzzling difficulties mothers face. That key is called "wisdom."

> Embedded in Scripture is an effective *strategy* for addressing all the real-life questions we have.

MOM, YOU NEED WISDOM!

Perhaps the most widely believed parenting fallacy in our culture is that love and good intentions are all it takes to be a good mother; if parents love their children and sacrifice enough, their children grow into healthy, productive adults. Many Christians believe this and support it with verses in the Bible that speak of the unsurpassed value of love for God and for others. Although love is an essential ingredient in good parenting, it is not sufficient (Prov. 24:3).

This message is very sobering for a mother. You can be completely devoted to your children and still fail miserably. Just because you are thinking of their best interest does not mean that your decisions are good for them. Love without godly wisdom can be a tragic recipe for disaster. Many well-meaning parents make terrible decisions for their children.

Fifteen-year-old Ashley was the apple of her parents' eye.

Certainly, they made decisions out of their genuine love for her. When prom came along, Ashley was thrilled to be invited to go with her eighteen-year-old boyfriend, the star of the basketball team. Her parents shared Ashley's excitement. They bought her a beautiful dress and paid for a day at the salon to get ready.

Although her curfew was 11:00, Ashley begged her parents to let her stay out late just this once. After all, the seniors were having a party that wouldn't even start until midnight. Ashley's parents relented and extended her curfew to 3:00 A.M.

Ashley stumbled through the door after 4:00 and had obviously been drinking. Throughout the next few days, Ashley tearfully relayed the sordid details of her first prom night. Her virginity was gone and her innocence lost.

Ashley's parents had made a loving decision. They only wanted to make their daughter happy. They had unselfishly spent over $400 on a dress, manicure and haircut. As pure as their motives were, they lacked wisdom.

Even godly men and women can make foolish parenting decisions. David clearly was sold out for God. He was a man after God's heart, yet his parenting was a disaster. The same can be said of the prophet Eli, who failed to discipline his sons. Jacob greatly loved his son Joseph. His thoughts often were occupied with how to make Joseph feel special. However, Jacob's love was not governed by wisdom. His love resulted in great pain and discord for Joseph and the rest of the family. Think of the many godly and devoted pastors and missionaries who have neglected wisdom in their own homes.

Proverbs 24:3–4 says, "By wisdom a house is built, and through understanding it is established; through knowledge its rooms are filled with rare and beautiful treasures." Proverbs 14:1 says, "The wise woman builds her house, but with her own hands the foolish one tears hers down." Wisdom—biblical wisdom—is the central principle of a blueprint for guilt-free motherhood. A mother whose parenting is rooted in godly wisdom parents proactively, pleasing God rather than reacting to her environment.

James 1:6–9 contrasts the lives of those who are committed to getting wisdom and those who doubt. James describes the doubters as a "wave of the sea, blown and tossed by the wind." He calls them "double-minded" and "unstable in all their ways."

Have you ever felt double-minded and unstable? I have. I can be tossed and blown so easily by the strongest pressure around me if I am not grounded in godly wisdom. My children's demands or the opinions of others determine my actions. Often, I parent based on my hunches or my gut. Even this approach has proven to be fickle and unreliable. I need a blueprint based on truth to ground my reactions and decisions as a mom.

GOD WANTS TO MAKE YOU WISE

Parenting with godly wisdom—is it attainable? Perhaps thinking about a blueprint for your mothering causes you to feel more inadequate. "How can I get wisdom? I thought this book was supposed to alleviate guilt, not add to it!"

So much of what is advertised in our culture is unattainable:

the perfect figures of models in magazines and actresses on television, the wealth promised through get-rich-quick schemes, eternal youth that exercise and healthy diets are supposed to guarantee. Live long enough, and you naturally become a skeptic of promised panaceas!

The Bible not only helps us direct our influence but also guarantees that we can have the resources to implement the advice. Unlike the empty promises of Fifth Avenue, God gives wisdom to any mother who is committed to godly parenting. He does not withhold wisdom from His children when they ask for it. He gives it generously.

If any of you lacks wisdom, he should ask God, who gives generously to all without finding fault, and it will be given to him.

(Jas. 1:5)

If you call out for insight and cry aloud for understanding . . . then you will understand the fear of the LORD and find the knowledge of God. For the LORD gives wisdom, and from his mouth come knowledge and understanding.

(Prov. 2:3, 5–6)

Every mom reading this book can become wise . . . can please God through her parenting. In fact, Paul writes to Christians in Corinth, "Brothers, think of what you were when you were called. Not many of you were wise by human standards . . . but God chose the foolish things of the world to shame the wise;

God chose the weak things of the world to shame the strong" (1 Cor. 1:26–27). Scripture is very clear about what we must do to be rooted in a blueprint of godly wisdom.

We Must Value Wisdom

> *Does not wisdom call out? Does not understanding raise her voice? On the heights along the way, where the paths meet, she takes her stand; beside the gates leading into the city, at the entrances, she cries aloud: "To you, O men, I call out; I raise my voice to all mankind. You who are simple, gain prudence; you who are foolish, gain understanding. . . . Choose my instruction instead of silver, knowledge rather than choice gold, for wisdom is more precious than rubies, and nothing you desire can compare with her."*
>
> (Prov. 8:1–5, 10–11)

Wisdom is available to whomever wants her. You don't have to be rich or smart to be wise. In fact, wisdom is actively seeking you. Like a three-year-old playing hide-and-seek, she abandons her hiding place and yells out, "Here I am! I want to be found!"

If wisdom is so easy to get, so readily available, then why is it also so rare? How few people ever find and embrace wisdom! In order to respond to wisdom's call, we must value her above what the world views as inherently valuable.

Undoubtedly the greatest example of God's gift of wisdom is the author of Proverbs, Solomon. "God gave Solomon wisdom and very great insight, and a breadth of understanding as measureless as the sand on the seashore" (1 Kgs. 4:29). What did Solomon do to deserve this wisdom? He asked for it, for the purpose of fulfilling God's task to him as king. Here is Solomon's prayer:

> *"Now, O LORD my God, you have made your servant king in place of my father David. But I am only a little child and do not know how to carry out my duties. Your servant is here among the people you have chosen, a great people, too numerous to count or number. So give your servant a discerning heart to govern your people and to distinguish between right and wrong. For who is able to govern this great people of yours?"*
>
> (1 Kgs. 3:7–9)

Sometimes my three little boys feel like "a great people" and I feel like "a little child" who does not know how to carry out my duties. Why don't I turn to the Lord, begging for wisdom and insight the way Solomon did? Read the Lord's answer to Solomon's humble prayer:

> *"Since you have asked for this and not for long life or wealth for yourself, nor have asked for the death of your enemies but for discernment in administering justice, I will do what you have asked. I will give you a wise and discerning heart, so that there will never have been anyone like you, nor will there ever be. Moreover, I will give you what you have not asked for—both riches and*

honor—so that in your lifetime you will have no equal among kings. And if you walk in my ways and obey my statutes and commands as David your father did, I will give you a long life."

(1 Kgs. 3:11–14)

Notice that God was not only pleased with what Solomon asked for, but also with what he did *not* ask for. Along with wisdom's cries in the street is a cacophony of competing advertisements promising happiness. Few place their trust in the promise of wisdom because we are so busy buying the world's recipe for success. You cannot seek both the world's approval and proactively seek God's plan for motherhood: "No one can serve two masters. Either he will hate the one and love the other, or he will be devoted to the one and despise the other" (Matt. 6:24).

Wisdom should not just be tacked onto the end of our grocery list of requests as an afterthought. Wisdom is our daily bread as mothers. We must realize that nothing we can ask for is more valuable to us or to our children. Paradoxically, we must surrender our pursuit of the things we believe bring success and happiness to truly receive God's gift of wisdom. Simply adding godly wisdom to your parenting paradigm only creates more guilt and anxiety. Wisdom is not meant to be a supplement, but the essence of a mother's focus. It is her survival.

> Wisdom is not meant to be a supplement, but the essence of a mother's focus. It is her survival.

Far too often, I fear that I am among those who foolishly run past wisdom in pursuit of the world's empty promises to me and my children. How humbling to realize the time I spend pursuing beauty, entertainment, accomplishments and material possessions for my children, only to pay token attention to the wisdom that can equip me as a mother.

Legend has it that the great teacher Socrates once was asked by a pupil, "How do I get wisdom?" Socrates answered the young man by leading him to the sea and walking him into the water. Socrates took his student by the shoulders and plunged him under the surface. Shocked and naturally frightened, the youth struggled as his teacher held his head under the water for what seemed like a lifetime. After more than a minute had passed, Socrates released his student, who emerged from the water gasping for air. His burning lungs were instantly relieved as he gulped the oxygen his body craved. The youth looked at his teacher with anger and confusion. *Maybe the old man has lost it,* he must have thought. Socrates then spoke to his student. "You want to be wise? When you long for wisdom the way your lungs ached for air, then wisdom will be yours."

> *Wisdom is supreme; therefore get wisdom. Though it cost you all you have, get understanding. Esteem her, and she will exalt you; embrace her and she will honor you.*
>
> (Prov. 4:7–8)

To get wisdom, we must want wisdom. We must want it so

badly that we are willing to ignore the world's demands and advice to us. As mothers drowning in a sea of confusion, we must plead for God's wisdom as we raise our children. Our hearts have to burn for wisdom the way our lungs burn for oxygen when deprived of it. It is indeed a great and endless treasure for weary mothers!

Throughout the book of Proverbs, wisdom is promised to those who search for her and seek her. Whereas receiving wisdom from God is passive, seeking her is our active responsibility. God is the source of all wisdom. He gives His children wisdom through the Holy Spirit when we ask. He has also provided other sources of wisdom that are available to those who "search for it as for hidden treasure" (Prov. 2:4).

Wisdom Is Found in God's Word

From the time of early childhood, I attended a wonderful church and was involved in many of the children's activities. I have had over thirty years of solid teaching from godly men and women, in addition to my own devotional time. As big as the Bible is, you would think I would have exhausted its content by this point in my life.

Sometimes, I get lazy and fall back on my many years of biblical knowledge rather than yearning for the wisdom of the Word of God. These days, free time is at a premium. About the only time I have to myself is roughly an hour before bedtime. I make a cup of tea and flop into my favorite reading chair. On the coffee table beside me are my *Newsweek* magazine (my only source of information from the outside world), usually one fiction and one nonfiction book I am in the middle of, and my Bible. The dilemma couldn't be any clearer to me. I know I *should* read my Bible, but I am so tired. I've spent all day doing the things I *should* do. It's my time! I want to read something fun and relaxing. I would be embarrassed to say how often I have chosen the book or magazine over the Bible.

The times that I do commit to really delving into God's Word (not just the obligatory quick read to ease my guilt), I am always amazed at the nourishment it provides. How could I have read the same portion so many times over my life, yet the words still leap off the page, hitting me square between the eyes! The words are so true—so filled with the wisdom I have been starved for all day. Why don't I long for my time in the Bible? Why are shallow books and depressing world news so much more appealing to me? I truly don't understand why something so rewarding is not naturally and easily my highest priority. How quickly I am deceived into believing that the world's recipe for rest and enjoyment can deliver!

I want to have the Psalmist's love for Scripture—to delight in the Law of the Lord. He understood how powerful and essential God's Word is to everything we do. I want to be able to genuinely say:

> *Oh, how I love your law! I meditate on it all day long.*
> *Your commands make me wiser than my enemies, for they*
> *are ever with me. I have more insight than all my teachers,*
> *for I meditate on your statutes. I have more understanding*

than the elders, for I obey your precepts. I have kept my feet from every evil path so that I might obey your word. I have not departed from your laws, for you yourself have taught me. How sweet are your words to my taste, sweeter than honey to my mouth!

(Ps. 119:97–103)

The Word of God is filled with wisdom! We can never exhaust the depth of God's wisdom revealed in Scripture. God's laws and precepts are true, and they will stand the test of time. Paul echoed this in his letter to Timothy, "All Scripture is God-breathed and is useful for teaching, rebuking, correcting and training in righteousness, so that the man of God may be thoroughly equipped for every good work" (2 Tim. 3:16–17).

Do you want to be thoroughly equipped as a mother? Begin your treasure hunt in the Word of God. You will be taught, challenged and trained in godly wisdom.

Wisdom Is Found in God's Creation

"I wish the Bible would tell me how to help my daughter with her eating disorder!" Although the Bible is our most valuable resource for seeking wisdom, it is not exhaustive. Millions of specific, personal and important questions are not answered within its pages. Just because it does not answer our questions does not mean the Bible is irrelevant to motherhood. What many fail to realize is that Scripture encourages us to find wisdom through a diligent study of God's creation. Everything that is, was made by Him—the Master Craftsman. God's wisdom is embedded in His creation and is available for us to examine and apply.

If you break your leg, you visit an orthopedic physician. That doctor has devoted many years to the study of the human body, bones in particular. As he treats your injury, he is applying the wisdom he has gained from studying God's creation. Even if he doesn't believe in God, he has access to the wisdom with which God created the human body. God has revealed His wisdom to all of us through His creation (Rom. 1:20).

The Bible encourages us to be students of God's wisdom, which, in fact, is the message of the entire book of Proverbs. Nowhere does God's plan for us become more practical than in Proverbs. This book deals head-on with real-life issues and questions: "A gentle answer turns away wrath, but a harsh word stirs up anger" (Prov. 15:1). The advice is practical and relevant enough to make the reader marvel at the fact that it was written thousands of years ago. A primary message of Proverbs is for us to study the cause-and-effect principles that God created and apply them to daily living.

God created humans to respond in certain predictable ways. How do people react to traumatic events? What is the best way to approach your spouse with a criticism? How do you convince your teenager not to sleep with her boyfriend? These questions all can and should be answered by studying God's creation, seeking His wisdom.

When a mom asks me, "How should I respond to my

daughter's temper tantrums?" I answer her based on my extensive study of how God created children in general (child psychology). Certain responses, like appeasing the child, are likely to encourage the tantrum. Other responses, such as isolating her, teach the child that her screaming will not be rewarded.

Although many view it as a God-forsaken field, psychology is a source of great wisdom *when approached correctly*. (Chapter 4 sheds light on how searching for wisdom can quickly turn into foolishness.) I pursue wisdom by studying and applying the principles of God's creation. Understanding how people respond to trauma, anger, affection, structure, encouragement and discipline helps me parent wisely.

Without realizing it, you probably glean from the wisdom of observation every day in your parenting. For example, your goal is for your three-year-old to eat broccoli. First, you try the airplane game. No "open sesame" here; her mouth stays glued shut. Next, you try bribing her with the promise of ice cream for dessert. Still she resists. Finally, out of frustration, you force the broccoli into her mouth. You bask in a brief moment of triumph until you notice the dreaded gag reflex. Next time you make broccoli, you know what not to do! After you melt some American cheese on the vegetable, suddenly your daughter starts to eat it. Congratulations! Your experience and observations have made you wise in the area of toddlers and vegetables.

As you astutely observe the predictable patterns of creation, you gain knowledge. When you apply those principles to your own circumstances, you become wise.

Proverbs, an excellent example of God-honoring psychology, is filled with illustrations of lessons gleaned from observations. As you read a few, notice how true Solomon's remarks are thousands of years later. The wisdom of God's creation has not changed!

Go to the ant, you sluggard; consider its ways and be wise! It has no commander, no overseer or ruler, yet it stores its provisions in summer and gathers its food at harvest.

(6:6–8)

A righteous man cares for the needs of his animal, but the kindest acts of the wicked are cruel.

(12:10)

He who works his land will have abundant food, but he who chases fantasies lacks judgment.

(12:11)

A heart at peace gives life to the body, but envy rots the bones.

(14:30)

Better a meal of vegetables where there is love than a fattened calf with hatred.

(15:17)

He who covers over an offense promotes love, but whoever repeats the matter separates friends.

(17:9)

An offended brother is more unyielding than a fortified city.

(18:19)

It is not good to have zeal without knowledge, nor to be hasty and miss the way.

(19:2)

Better to live in a desert than with a quarrelsome and ill-tempered wife.

(21:19—I can hear my husband saying "Amen!")

If a man loudly blesses his neighbor early in the morning, it will be taken as a curse.

(27:14)

How about a book of Proverbs for mothers? We could certainly write our own proverbs from what we have learned through experience or observation. How about these?

Dirty laundry is like manna; no matter how many baskets full you collect, more is sure to fall from the sky tomorrow.

The stench of an open Diaper Genie could qualify as a weapon of mass destruction.

If you hate feeling guilty, avoid Creative Memories parties.

As fingernails are to a chalkboard, so is the sound of Baby Bop's voice.

Throw away your child's Happy Meals toys and crafts only when the kids are in bed; bury them deep down in the trash can.

You don't want to know how much your child's kindergarten teacher knows about your family!

Never say the words "fat," "ugly," or "bald" within earshot of young children. They are sure to be repeated in the most embarrassing circumstances.

When you get to the doctor's office, your child's symptoms will magically disappear.

As mothers, we can relate to these proverbs because in the process of raising our kids, we have experienced many of the same things. These examples are humorous, but gaining wisdom can inform our critical parenting decisions as well. What can you do to encourage your child's confidence? How can you squelch sibling rivalry? How do you help your child survive teasing and rejection? How do you point her in the right career direction? The list is endless; but wisdom is up to the task! She can inform and equip you in any parenting dilemma you face!

Develop a Council of Wise Advisors

Through attentive study of God's Word and His creation, unending wisdom can be ours. However, you and I have limited time and energy. We cannot seek out all the treasures of wisdom. No one can become an expert in all areas. There are very practical limitations to the amount of wisdom that we can glean, which is why Proverbs tells us to seek wise counsel.

Physicians, architects, pastors, bankers, psychologists, parents, friends, lawyers, scientists, teachers, accountants, consultants and plumbers are just some of the experts who may sit on your panel of personal wise counselors. Throughout parenting, you run up against questions that you cannot answer and problems that overwhelm you. In addition to prayer and personal study, seek the resources that God has provided through experts who are gifted in particular areas of knowledge.

The quality of the advice you seek is crucial to being wise. If you do not use discretion in choosing advisors, you may get terrible advice. Just because someone is knowledgeable in one area does not necessarily make them a good advisor in another. My children's pediatrician is a reliable medical advisor, but I do not seek her advice concerning spiritual areas. My mechanic can fix my car, but I would never ask him to cut my hair.

How do you know if a counselor is wise? When an issue involves moral or spiritual dimensions, be assured that your counselor is committed to God's authority! No matter how good the advice sounds, true wisdom never contradicts godly principles. Additionally, test the fruits of others when

> No matter how good the advice sounds, true wisdom never contradicts godly principles.

seeking wise counselors. Are fruits of wisdom evident in their lives?

Some of your most dependable and accessible counselors may not be professionals in any field. Mentors, parents, siblings and friends may be tremendous resources of wisdom because they know you, your spouse and your children so well. When one of my kids is acting up, I usually rely on my sister or mother to give me some insight into what they have observed. They know what's normal for my family and what is not. Close friends and family members are also willing to tell me the truth, even when it hurts.

A fine line exists between seeking wise counsel and parenting based on the approval of others. One is a tool of proactive parenting while the other is reacting. The wisdom of others should inform, never determine, your decisions.

Wisdom is there for the asking. Wisdom is available to those who seek her, but God's wisdom is only life-changing when we lean on her to build our homes. Here is how Jesus concluded the Sermon on the Mount in Matthew 7:24–27:

> *Therefore, everyone who hears these words of mine and puts them into practice is like a wise man who built his house on the rock. The rain came down, the streams rose, and the winds blew and beat against that house; yet it did not fall, because it had its foundation on the rock. But everyone who hears these words of mine and does not put them into practice is like a foolish man who built his house on sand. The rain came down, the streams rose, and the winds blew and beat against that house, and it fell with a great crash.*

Because I am a psychologist, people come to see me when the rains come, the streams rise and the winds blow . . . tragedy, conflict, great loss, anxiety, failure and rejection. I have seen women who build their houses wisely on the rock and those who haphazardly ignore wisdom, building their priceless homes upon the sand. I have seen lives withstand remarkable storms, and I have seen others fall with a great crash. No mother wants to end with a crash, engulfed by the guilt of foolishness.

> *Blessed is the man who finds wisdom, the man who gains understanding, for she is more profitable than silver and yields better return than gold. She is more precious than rubies; nothing you desire can compare with her. Long life is in her right hand; in her left hand are riches and honor. Her ways are pleasant ways, and all her paths are peace. She is the tree of life to those who embrace her; those who lay hold of her will be blessed.*
>
> (Prov. 3:13–18)

If you choose to begin building your family based on a blueprint of godly wisdom, read on. We delve into the nuts and bolts of God's wise instruction for us as mothers. Wisdom begins with the fear of the Lord, continues with basic principles of value and concludes with acknowledging the limits of a mother's influence.

How much better to get wisdom than gold,
to choose understanding than silver!

Proverbs 16:16

For Personal Reflection

1. Is it difficult for you to think of motherhood as a ministry or call-ing? Why or why not?

_____

_____

2. Up until this point, have you had a "blueprint" for motherhood? If so, what is it?

_____

_____

3. Read Proverbs 8:1–5 and 9:1–6. Do you believe wisdom is seeking you?

_____

_____

4. What distracts you from seeking and yielding to wisdom?

_____

_____

Wisdom for Dummies

I recently had a conversation with a woman who had a very strong reaction when she heard that I was a psychologist. "I don't mean your profession any disrespect," she said, "but a counselor almost ruined my marriage." She had my attention. "A few years ago, my husband and I were having some marital problems, so we went to a counselor whom a friend had recommended. He seemed like a nice guy, had the right credentials and even attended our church. Naturally, we trusted his advice. Six months into counseling, we began to realize that this expert's recommendations were making matters worse. He encouraged us each to keep secrets from each other, downplayed my husband's involvement with pornography and generally fueled the resentment we had between us. The damage took years to undo."

What went wrong with this couple? They were seeking wisdom. Why didn't their search for help heal their marriage? Unfortunately, not all wisdom is created equally. In fact, much of the advice the average person finds is really foolishness parading as wisdom.

Although our society is filled with outlets of advice, truth is a rare gem. Even though many around us want wisdom, few ever find it. The world has ignored and scoffed at the absolutely essential and foundational ingredient for wisdom: the fear of the Lord.

As part of his residency in orthopedic surgery, a friend of mine had to do a rotation in obstetrics and gynecology. Dave and his fellow residents were preparing to deliver their first babies, surely a terrifying and magnificent experience for any young man. They awaited the coaching of their supervising physician, wondering how to ease the suffering of the laboring moms and how to safely bring these new lives into the world. His instructions were simple, yet profound, "Most important: just don't drop the baby!"

Often, we can be so absorbed with the advanced lessons of life that we overlook the foundational fundamentals. In our quest for wisdom as mothers, we must begin where God tells us is the very beginning: the fear of the Lord. At fifteen places, the writer of Proverbs talks about the "fear of the Lord." Fearing the Lord is cited four times as the foundation of wisdom. The concept of fearing God is mentioned in at least twenty-two other books of the Bible. The fear of the Lord certainly appears to be a central theme for followers of Christ, but one that is easily skipped over.

"The fear of the LORD is the beginning of wisdom" (Prov. 9:10). Most of us have heard or read that phrase a multitude of times. It's pretty simple, right? Like "just don't drop the baby." The implication is that if we seek knowledge and wisdom but don't fear God, our searching is in vain. Do we really understand what it means to fear the Lord?

To Fear or Not to Fear

Most people do not spend much energy fearing God because it is such a vague directive. How do you fear the Lord? We can get our arms around passages that tell us not to gossip, complain or engage in immorality. Although we don't always do it, we know how to treat others with kindness, forgiveness and compassion. But fear the Lord? What does that look like? Fear is an emotion, not an action, right? Does God really want us to be afraid of Him?

Learning to fear God is also confusing because throughout Scripture, we see glimpses of a loving and compassionate God. Didn't Jesus hold the little children? Isn't God presented as an approachable Father?

The character of God is so infinite that our minds cannot grasp all of who He is. Sometimes it is difficult to reconcile God's wrath and judgment with His love and mercy. How could God kill Ananias and Sapphira (Acts 5:1–11) for their lies, yet offer such compassion and mercy to the woman caught in adultery (John 8)? Is He ultimately a God of mercy or a God of judgment?

To fear the Lord can mean to be afraid of His judgment. Reading through the book of Revelation or a quick trip through most Old Testament books drives home the truth that surely it is a frightful thing to "fall into the hands of an angry God." However, fearing the Lord means more than just dreading punishment. Christians are called to have a holy fear of God. *The New Bible Dictionary* (Wheaton, Ill.: Tyndale House Publishers, Inc., 1962) calls it "God-given, enabling men to reverence God's authority, obey his commandments, and hate and shun all forms of evil."

Sadly, we live in a time and place that has no understanding of the fear of the Lord. God's name is carelessly kicked around like a hacky sack. His character is defamed and blasphemed regularly on television and in movies. We sit back and laugh, marginalizing the holiness of God—forgetting the warnings that these sins will not go unpunished.

When was the last time you trembled at God's power? were in awe of His holiness? felt fear from His righteousness? turned away from sin because of His judgment?

Yes, God is our friend. He is merciful. Christ has paid for sin. But we must not lose our reverence for God. We must not take His holiness flippantly. Imagine what it will be like to see Him split the sky on a white horse with trumpets blaring and His angels at His side! what it will be like to stand before Him, all secrets revealed—to be face-to-face with the Creator and Lord of the universe! *We fear the Lord when we recognize that He alone is God. His power and glory are unsurpassed!*

Fearing the Lord is the critical element that distinguishes godly wisdom from worldly wisdom, which God calls foolishness (1 Cor. 1:19–20). How do you know if advice is sound? Judge it by the plumb line of the fear of the Lord. *Wisdom cannot be truly wise if it violates the fear of the Lord!*

ONLY GOD'S DOMAIN

Throughout Scripture, the fear of the Lord is linked to morality and obeying the standards that God has laid before us. Those who fear the Lord turn from evil (Prov. 3:7; 8:13). Those who do not fear the Lord are prone toward wickedness. In Psalm 36:1–3, King David tells us:

> *"An oracle is within my heart concerning the sinfulness of the wicked: There is no fear of God before his eyes. For in his own eyes he flatters himself too much to detect or hate his sin. The words of his mouth are wicked and deceitful; he has ceased to be wise and to do good."*

The fear of the Lord is the beginning of wisdom. To not fear the Lord is the beginning of all sin. God is the absolute definer of good and evil. Our knowledge of good and evil must come directly and without question from Him. To fear the Lord means that we recognize His total moral authority and the consequences of defying that authority. "But that's so narrow!" the "wise" in our culture scream. If you refer to the Bible as the moral reference, you are regarded as a fool.

Abortion, little white lies, extramarital sex, divorce apart from biblical grounds, cheating on income taxes . . . we can form sophisticated arguments that justify all of these decisions. Yet, the very moment we begin to question God's moral authority and create our own standards of good and evil, we are sliding down a dangerous slope of foolishness.

Christians are often called arrogant for their narrow and rigid definition of morality. However, refusing to question God's absolute authority is not pride, but humility. It is impossible to fear the Lord appropriately and be arrogant. Bible-believing Christians are not the definers of morality; they only recognize that God is. Furthermore, only because of the grace of God can any man or woman escape the pride of humanity and yield to God's authority (1 Cor. 1:26–31).

God has given us a worldwide garden to learn and discover and in which to seek wisdom. If we had one hundred lifetimes, we could still not exhaust the knowledge and wisdom of His creation. But in the midst of exploring and tasting of the garden, He has instructed us to not eat from the tree in the middle of the garden—the tree of the knowledge of good and evil. We are never to become the definers of morality, and it is tempting. Sometimes God's morality doesn't make sense. It seems narrow and unfair. But God is God. We have no right to question or reinvent His moral authority. This is the beginning of wisdom.

WHY FEAR OF THE LORD IS KEY TO PARENTING

So, what in the world does this have to do with parenting? Not only is the fear of the Lord related to parenting, to a mother it is foundational to honoring God. Proverbs 14:26 says, "He who fears the LORD has a secure fortress, and for his children it will be a refuge."

As moms, we are faced with very difficult parenting decisions. As we seek wisdom to parent wisely, fearing the Lord keeps us safely within the parameters of God's will for us and our children. Any time we fail to revere God, we are playing with fire. What seems like wisdom can quickly become foolishness.

"My son is sixteen years old," a client explained. "Of course, we want him to stay sexually pure, but let's face it: Most of his friends are having sex. We really don't want him to get his girlfriend pregnant or get a disease, so we are encouraging him to use condoms *if* he has sex, which we told him not to do."

At one level, this argument makes sense. But do you see the foolishness in teaching a child to fear God, yet making provisions for if he doesn't? What message is this parent really sending about his ability to keep God's standards? They are actually trying to help him avoid the consequences of sins he has not yet committed!

A lot of parenting advice is out there—books, seminars, talk shows on television. Usually, one source of advice completely contradicts another source. Whose advice is wise and whose is not? The first question to ask yourself when sifting through

> The first question to ask yourself when sifting through wisdom is, "Does this advice support or conflict with God's authority?"

wisdom is, "Does this advice support or conflict with God's authority?" Many of today's cultural parenting problems are the direct result of our lax attitude toward God's authority. Without the conviction of godly standards and a biblical mandate for parenting, moms become wishy-washy with their own authority.

Fearing the Lord Is the Foundation of Respect for Authority

A mother is grocery shopping with her six-year-old son. "Mom, I want Cocoa Krispies for breakfast," the boy demands.

"No, honey. Cocoa Krispies are not healthy. How about Frosted Mini-Wheats? You like those."

"No, I want Cocoa Krispies!" screams the boy as he throws two boxes of the cereal in the cart.

The mom's face turns red as she obediently wheels the cart filled with her son's desired goodies.

What's wrong with this picture? This boy has no respect for his mother's authority. The mom fears her son's temper tantrums or disapproval far more than he fears her discipline. Soon, the conflict will not be over cereal choice, but what the boy watches on television, whom he dates, what language he uses and how he responds to peer pressure. She may advise, cajole and plead for him to make wise choices, but he has learned at a young age to be his own boss.

Our society seems to have lost practically all respect for authority. Teachers, policemen, lawmakers and judges are viewed as corrupt or at best incompetent. Parents garner their children's obedience through bribes and threats, because respect is a relic of the past. If a kid can get away with something, it's not wrong.

The fear of the Lord is the basis of all respect for authority—including a parent's. Without an absolute standard of right and wrong, we make moral decisions based on circumstances. If there is no ultimate accounting for our behavior, we obey only when it is in our immediate best interest. If a mother has no respect for God's authority, how can her child respect her position? What is the basis of her parenting mandate? Her kids may listen to her when it serves their best interest, but their obedience will be circumstantial—not based on principle.

> *"Mom, can I go see* Daredevil *this weekend?" asks ten-year-old Anne.*
>
> *"What is it rated, Anne?" her mother inquires.*
>
> *"I think it's PG-13. But it's not bad! All my friends are going. Hannah's mom is taking us."*
>
> *"I don't like you to see 13s," replies Mom.*
>
> *"Mom! Why can't I see it when every other ten-year-old in the world has seen it? All their moms say it's okay!"*

Anne is questioning the basis of her mom's decision. A mother grounded in Scripture would respond: "God has given me the job of raising you. He gave *me* that job—not Hannah's mother. I am in charge of monitoring what kind of movies you watch. The review says *Daredevil* is rated PG-13 due to 'violence, language, and mild sexuality.' These are not things that honor God. Therefore, I will not allow you to see it. End of story."

If Anne's mother cannot refer to God's moral authority, her parenting decisions will seem arbitrary. Why is a thirteen-year-old allowed to see "violence, language and sexuality" when a ten-year-old is not?

Referring to God's authority in your life communicates to your children that you are responsible for your conduct as a mother. Your decisions are not based on your opinion or emotions but are rooted in your own reverence for and devotion to God.

Fearing the Lord Encourages Lasting Values

God's authority also instills in children moral standards that eventually supersede their parents' rules. Someday, Anne will be eighteen. She will see whatever movies she likes. She will no longer rely upon her mother's standards to judge right from wrong. What authority will replace her mother's? If Anne's mother has taught her to fear the Lord, any movie Anne chooses to see must be measured against the yardstick of God's standards. Although she may still make bad choices, she will do so with the knowledge that she is accountable to God.

What movies a kid sees may seem like a somewhat harmless

issue. But how do you stop your teenager from having sex with her boyfriend when you can't be there all the time to chaperone? How do you keep your son from cheating on an exam in college? How do you teach him to be kind to a stranger or tell the truth when no one is looking? If your moral authority as a parent is not rooted in fearing the Lord, fat chance your children will incorporate the same morality when they are no longer in your care! When they no longer fear being grounded, spanked or reprimanded, what is to keep them from evil?

When your parenting is rooted in godly standards, you teach your children *self-discipline*. They learn to refer to biblical standards when making decisions. Gradually, they begin to incorporate the fear of the Lord into their own thinking. Ultimately, it is not your authority, but their respect for God's authority, that keeps your kids from wrongdoing.

SO, HOW DO I FEAR GOD IN MOTHERHOOD?

Fearing God sure sounds like a heavy topic! How does an overwhelmed mother find time in her day to instill in her children a reverence for the Lord? Fortunately, the average day affords moms countless opportunities to teach children to revere God. Fearing God is not an event or an occasional statement, but is rather a lifestyle choice.

Listed below are a few practical areas in which we can demonstrate and teach our children the beginning of wisdom. As you read these, keep in mind that God's righteousness and majesty stand uncompromised by His immeasurable love. Both His judgment and mercy are true without canceling out each other. Perhaps the most challenging job of a mother is creating a parenting atmosphere in which our children can experience the fear of the Lord along with His unfailing love.

Showing Reverence

Growing up, it seemed that my family was at church whenever the doors were opened. Sunday school, worship service, Sunday night service, midweek service, youth retreats, Bible camp—you name it. We rarely missed church. While at church, we had to walk, not run. If we attended the worship service, we had to sit quietly and listen. The church bulletin always had a picture of our pastor in it. One Sunday, during the service, my sister and I had a contest to see who could make the pastor's picture look funnier. She penciled in a mustache, beard, and goofy glasses. I took it a step further and drew horns on his head and vampire teeth in his mouth. When my parents saw what we had done, they made us go up to the pastor and apologize—*and* we had to show him our artwork! My parents were certainly strict when it came to honoring God in church. Although our behavior was just kids being kids, they had little tolerance for foolishness.

When I went to college, I remember relishing the freedom of making my own decisions about church. I could wear jeans and a sweatshirt to church if I wanted to. If the sermon were boring, I could bring a book to read or write notes to my friends. I didn't even have to go to church if I didn't feel like it. Many Sundays I chose to sleep in instead. We joked about going to "Bedside Baptist" and listening to "Pastor Pillow." Sunday was just another day to catch up on sleep or studies. At the time, I viewed the weekly ritual of dressing up and spending Sundays at church as legalistic and unnecessary. After all, I could love God and have a rich devotional life without regular church attendance.

I developed the same attitude towards prayer. As kids we would fold our hands, close our eyes and bow our heads whenever we prayed. At bedtime, we knelt by our beds to thank the Lord for our blessings and ask for His protection. Prior to every meal, we prayed before anyone took a bite of food. As I "matured," I relaxed these rituals. I realized that there is no "magic" in praying before meals. And I could pray just as effectively with my eyes opened as with them closed. Why kneel by my bed when I could comfortably pray lying down?

Now that I have children, I have gained a new appreciation for teaching spiritual disciplines. I see my children whispering or sneaking bites of food during prayer. I hear them complaining about having to dress up and "waste play time" at church on Sunday. I notice their prayers are rushed and meaningless. I wonder if they are learning to fear the Lord. Do they understand the privilege it is to worship and talk to their Creator?

I want to show the Lord reverence, and I desperately want my children to respect Him. How I approach church, prayer, the Word of God and communion all demonstrate my fear of God. They are tangible ways to teach my kids that God is awesome and worthy of our greatest respect.

Perhaps the most important way of showing reverence for the Lord is the way in which we use His name. Of all the evil deeds God could have included in the commandments, He chose this one to be among the ten: "You shall not misuse the name of the LORD your God" (Deut. 5:11). God takes this so seriously that He added a caveat at the end of this particular commandment, "for the LORD will not hold anyone guiltless who misuses his name." Murder, theft, adultery, no other commandment has such a warning attached to it!

Misuse of God's name has become so socially acceptable that most people don't even realize they do it. It's hard to go through a day without hearing someone flip His name around like a common noun or conversation filler. There are a lot of raunchy words our kids can say, but nothing is worse than taking the Lord's name in vain. Some parents feel so strongly about revering God's name that they prohibit their children from using slang versions like, "Geez," or "Oh my gosh."

As parents, we set the standards for the behavior in our homes. Although children may not understand or appreciate disciplines that demonstrate respect for God, they will learn them as we highlight their importance. Prayer, attending church and "saying the right words" are meaningless without a sincere trust in God. Ritual without relationship becomes legalism. However, as our children develop their own relationship with Christ, the disciplines they learned in childhood become valuable vehicles to guide and direct their faith.

Draw Lines of Authority and Boundaries

The first four of the Ten Commandments address revering God. The fifth commandment is perhaps an extension: "Honor your father and your mother" (Deut. 5:16). In Romans 13, Paul writes that we are to submit to all authority because every earthly authority is ultimately rooted in God. The parent-child relationship is a direct metaphor of a Christian's relationship with God. Without question, children learn to approach God based on their interactions with their parents.

Friendship parenting is a pretty common trend these days. Parents want their children to view them as friends, people they could talk to as easily as their peers. Parents who embrace this philosophy try to dress cool and use the hip terms of their kids' generation. They want to relate to their children. These parents also try to limit the restrictions they place on their kids. After all, too many rules and you might be labeled old-fashioned. Even worse, your kids might get mad at you or not share their secrets with you.

Nothing is wrong with having fun with your kids. There should be plenty of times to tickle, play games, tell jokes and make fun memories. Parents and children can develop bonds of deep friendship over the years. However, parenting based primarily on friendship undermines healthy authority. Although friendship parents generally have admirable motives, their parenting lacks the critical element of boundaries. Kids have other friends; they don't have other parents. Parents are the most significant authority figure children have. Parents must maintain their authority, even when doing so is unpopular or unpleasant. How can children ever learn to respect and submit to God's absolute authority when every other authority is questioned?

In too many homes, the boundaries between parent and child, adults and children, is blurred. Gone are the days when children refer to adults as "Mr." and "Mrs." No longer are kids taught to ask permission to have a cookie. When a directive is given, kids don't respond with "Yes, sir" or "Yes, ma'am" but with "Why?" or "I don't want to." The focus is on bonding to the exclusion of discipline. Respecting authority is a very biblical concept and is part and parcel of teaching kids to fear the Lord. Training our children to treat parents, teachers, pastors, police officers and adults in general with respect will serve them well.

On the opposite extreme of the parenting paradigm, some moms go overboard with their authority. In an effort to maintain order and respect, they crush the spirit and dignity of their children. Sustaining boundaries does not mean that parents have to be harsh, abrasive, critical or rigid with their children. Their discipline and decisions can be firm, yet loving and edifying. As Tedd Tripp suggests in his book, *Shepherding Your Child's Heart,* a home should be a "benevolent dictatorship." Children are valued and their opinions are solicited, but they need to know they are not in charge. Research has consistently shown that the most effective parents are those who instill a high degree of both love and discipline in their homes.

Kids who have too much power or say-so at home are generally more anxious than children who can rest in their parents' authority. It is comforting for a child to have limits and structure that are reinforced by their parents. Many times in counseling, parents complain that their children are unruly and hyperactive at home but well-behaved in school. Kids respond well to routine and boundaries. Although they are rarely able or willing to voice this, it is comforting to know that Mom and Dad are strong enough to impose and enforce limits. In the same way, Christians can rest in knowing the safety of living within God's will.

Maintaining boundaries of respect with your children is difficult, especially when you are with them all day. Some evenings when my husband comes home from work, he notices that the boys are unresponsive to my instruction. Often, I don't even realize that it takes five requests to get them to obey or that I am rewarded with a rolling of the eyes when I correct them. I have fought the battle all day. I just get worn down. I want to have fun with my kids, and I don't always want to be correcting them. However, respect is like exercise; it's a lot easier to stay in shape than it is to get back in shape after letting yourself slide. Having a loving, fun and peaceful home depends upon establishing and maintaining healthy parental boundaries.

Teach Biblical Standards

Moses had just delivered the Ten Commandments to the Israelites. Then he said:

> *"These are the commands, decrees and laws the* Lord *your God directed me to teach you to observe in the land that you*

are crossing the Jordan to possess, so that you, your children,
and their children after them may fear the Lord *your God*
as long as you live by keeping all his decrees and commands
that I give you, and so that you may enjoy long life. . . .
These commandments that I give to you today are to be
upon your hearts. Impress them on your children. Talk
about them when you sit at home and when you walk along
the road, and when you lie down and when you get up."

(Deut. 6:1–2, 6–7)

This statement was God's prescription for the Israelites as they were going into a very pagan culture. Parents were instructed to daily and consistently teach God's law to their children, which would ensure a heritage of fearing God and devotion to Him.

Teaching our children biblical standards of right and wrong anchors them to the fear of the Lord. Memorizing Scripture, reading Bible stories and family devotions are all disciplines that impress the Word of God on the hearts of our children. It is impossible to daily and sincerely study the Bible and not have respect for God! From David and Goliath to the Holy Spirit's power in the early church, the Bible tells the story of an active and awesome Savior.

Living in a pluralistic culture that frowns on absolute truths, many parents shy away from declaring what the Bible teaches. Not wanting to appear too dogmatic, they respond to their children's questions with political correctness. Instead of stating biblical truth, they may couch their answers with qualifications

like, "Some people believe this, and others believe that." What a
tragic error! Our culture's disrespect for truth does not make the
Bible any less true. We do our children a great injustice when we
are cowardly about our faith. Yes, we don't have all the answers.
But God, through Scripture, has given us many of them. We
know about heaven, hell, God and the evil one. We know right
and wrong. Increasingly so, our beliefs put us and our children
at odds with the culture. Someday my children will ask me
about the gay lifestyle, abortion, and whether or not "good"
people go to heaven even if they don't know Jesus. Do I teach
them political correctness, or do I teach them to seek the truth
that is rooted in the Bible?

Has not the Lord called us to "be in this world but not of it"?
Didn't he remind us that we are aliens and that the world would
hate us because of Christ? The world (or at least some in it) may
hate our children because we have taught them truth. Although
this fact may cause temporary discomfort and even conflict, the
Bible says, "What good will it be for a man if he gains the whole
world, yet forfeits his soul?" (Matt. 16:26). Nothing is more
important than teaching our children to trust God's righteousness and to revere His holiness.

The best way to teach right from wrong is to refer to the Bible
when you or your children are faced with moral decisions—
whether to tell on a friend who was cheating in school, what to
do with money you found on the sidewalk, how to respond to a
bully or how to treat other children. Your fourteen-year-old
daughter is knee-deep in the world of junior-high cliques. Her

best friend hasn't quite garnered the acceptance of the "in" crowd. As you talk to your daughter about the situation, encourage her to seek and reflect on biblical principles. What does the Bible say about friendship? gossip? excluding others? pride? Instead of giving her the answers, challenge her with the questions.

A friend of ours, Rob, took his five-year-old daughter to lunch with him one day. The server accidentally gave him $10 extra in change after the bill had been paid. Instead of simply returning the money, Rob took the opportunity to teach his daughter about integrity. "Darcie, the lady gave us too much money back. What do you think we should do with it?" he asked. "We could use it to play video games or go to a movie, or we could give it back to the lady. What do you think God would want us to do?" Rob's question prompted a discussion with his daughter about stealing and honesty. Parenting is filled with such opportunities to teach our children to apply the Bible to decision making.

Consequences for Misbehavior

Along with learning right from wrong, parents also have to teach their children that making poor choices results in negative consequences. Sin often brings pleasure and success for a season. The Bible assures us that there will someday be judgment for wickedness. But often sin seems to pay satisfying dividends. In the here and now, people lie, cheat and hurt others to prosper. Seeing other children get away with (and even be rewarded for) bad behavior makes our kids doubt the standards of morality that we try to teach. Solomon reflects on this problem in Ecclesiastes 8:11: "When the sentence for a crime is not quickly carried out, the hearts of the people are filled with schemes to do wrong."

A woman comes to counseling troubled by fear of flying on airplanes. The most effective way to address her phobia is to expose her to what she fears. First, she would be asked to imagine getting in an airplane. Over time, the imagery would become more and more detailed as she learns to master her anxiety. The woman would then be encouraged to go to the airport. The next step might be for her to sit in an airplane. Finally, she would actually fly in the plane. The more often she flies on airplanes and lands safely, the less her fear controls her. Each uneventful flight proves her fear to be unfounded. Likewise, if you sin and do not experience negative consequences, you learn to no longer fear negative consequences.

Sometimes my kids lie about really insignificant things, like what they ate for lunch. Sometimes they disobey me on issues that don't really matter, like taking their shoes off when they get in the house. However, if I overlook lying or disobedience on the little issues, they learn to no longer fear punishment. In other situations, their honesty and obedience are paramount. When I tell them to hold my hand in a busy parking lot, obedience protects them from harm. Therefore, I must consistently respond to misbehavior, even on the little things.

Lying or disobeying God rarely has immediate consequences. A parent's job is to create immediate consequences that reflect the harm that eventually results from foolish choices. Proverbs

> A parent's job is to create immediate consequences that reflect the harm that eventually results from foolish choices.

3:12 says, "The Lord disciplines those he loves, as a father the son he delights in."

I hate to discipline my kids. Seeing them sad really hurts me, but Mike and I must teach our boys that disobedience results in punishment. If we are lax and allow them to finagle their way around "justice," they naturally apply this lesson to their relationship with God. The Lord takes disobedience and rebellion seriously! So must we.

Modeling Reverence

Perhaps the most important aspect of teaching our children the fear of the Lord is our own example. Do your kids know that you, too, are accountable to God's standards of right and wrong? As you parent, do they recognize that you make decisions in deference to God's authority?

A parent or grandparent who fears the Lord truly is a fortress for children. Even through rebellious times, children recall the image of their mother kneeling by the bedside. They remember the words of Scripture flowing from the speech of a beloved grandmother. They cannot shake the testimony of a father who refused to compromise biblical standards.

The single element that separates true wisdom from God-honoring wisdom is the fear of the Lord. If you are trying to model wisdom without living in reverence to God, give it up now. You will fail. No matter how noble your motive and how vast your efforts, seeking wisdom without fear of the Lord is inevitably fruitless. Reverence for God's holiness is the rock upon which all wisdom stands. Without it, you become as a god for your children; you define right and wrong; you declare truth. Fear of the Lord is the foundation of guilt-free motherhood, forcing us to relinquish illusions of wisdom and claims of ownership of our children. Fearing God cements our parenting in the unchanging, unwavering and trustworthy truth of our Creator.

Remember, "Don't drop the baby!" Motherhood is complicated. Finding the resources to become a wise mother can be daunting. But in our quest for wisdom, let's not skip past one of the most wonderful gifts we can give our children: a mother who fears the Lord.

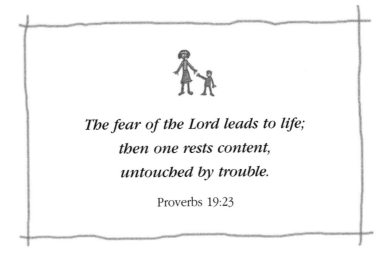

The fear of the Lord leads to life;
then one rests content,
untouched by trouble.

Proverbs 19:23

For Personal Reflection

1. Why is the fear of the Lord the beginning of wisdom for you as a mother?

   _____

   _____

2. Honestly evaluate your own attitudes and behaviors. In what ways do you model a reverence for God? respect for authority?

   _____

   _____

3. How do you balance teaching your children to fear God with teaching them to trust His love? How do your relationships with your children demonstrate this balance?

   _____

   _____

4. What ground rules, traditions, or disciplines in your home teach your children a reverence for God's authority?

   _____

   _____

5

The Seven Parenting Pillars of Wisdom

I have never been one for picture-taking. With a stroller, diaper bag, purse and wiggly kids to cart around, who needs the hassle of a camera and extra rolls of film? Whenever the kids would do something cute at home, the camera was never handy. When I grabbed for it, it was usually out of film or had a dead battery. Life is too busy for picture-taking. I used to get aggravated when my husband, Mike, insisted on bringing a camera and video recorder on everyday outings like swimming, T-ball games and school events. I really thought it was a waste of time and money. The developed pictures would get thrown into boxes of memorabilia to collect dust.

My attitude changed when my sister introduced me to the amazing world of scrapbooking. She took me to a shop with albums, walls of decorated paper, stickers for every event imaginable and tools that cut pictures in hundreds of different shapes. When we arrived back at my sister's house with my first scrapbooking materials, my brother-in-law rolled his eyes. "Oh, no!" he joked. "Now you're hooked. Next she'll introduce you to her Creative Memories dealer whom you'll be calling at odd hours of the night to get your scrapbooking fix!"

He was right! Capturing my children's fleeting childhood has become addictive! At first, I was overwhelmed. My oldest was already five. How would I catch up on all the years of his life I had wasted not scrapbooking? As I compulsively began to sort through pictures, I couldn't believe all of the important events and everyday photo ops I had missed over the years. If it hadn't been for Mike, I would have had to draw pictures of what my children looked like as babies!

My picture-taking habits have been completely transformed. Now I always have a camera ready within arm's reach. Not only that, but I find myself searching for great pictures. When we go somewhere, I save ticket stubs and brochures. Scrapbooking has made such a dramatic change in my picture-taking attitude because it has given me a reason to take pictures. I now imagine creative ways of chronicling birthdays, milestones, trips and everyday memories. No longer are my pictures stored in dusty boxes, but they are artfully cropped and framed (at least in theory!).

We become energized at a task when we have a sense of direction and purpose. Guilt-free mothering is parenting with the purpose outlined by godly wisdom. Each day represents not simply a sequence of random events, but opportunities to artfully craft our children's character. But how does purpose translate into effective parenting? How do we even define our purpose? The writer of Proverbs begins his book of wisdom by outlining the purpose of his writing:

> . . . for attaining wisdom and discipline; for understanding words of insight; for acquiring a disciplined and prudent life, doing what is right and just and fair; for giving prudence to the simple, knowledge and discretion to the young.
>
> (Prov. 1:2–4)

The purpose of Proverbs is to disciple and teach wisdom. It sounds like a job description for parents. In fact, in several places the author begins instruction with "My son." Although lessons on parenting are sprinkled throughout the Bible, the lessons and wisdom of Proverbs directly relate to our task of parenting. Proverbs helps define a mother's purpose.

In the last chapter we explored the fear of the Lord as the beginning of wisdom. While the fear of the Lord is the foundation of your blueprint, the Bible gives us many more principles to keep in focus as we build. As you read Proverbs, notice additional major themes of advice that seem to appear over and over again. In fact, Solomon can seem downright repetitive in his advice, like a mother saying for the hundredth time, "Chew with your mouth closed!" Like pages in a scrapbook, these seven themes can help give purpose to our influence as we strive to raise our children with wisdom:

Productivity
Uncompromising Integrity
Restrained Speech
Positive Relationships
Openness to Feedback
Self-Control
Eye to the Future

Each of these themes is a characteristic of maturity. They help us focus our influence by setting very specific goals for our children's development. These seven character traits can turn normal, everyday interactions and decisions into opportunities for you to be faithful to God's call to wisdom. As you strive to fulfill God's purpose for you as a mother, your influence will be wisely spent, not squandered.

These seven traits may seem overwhelming to you. They may highlight areas that you have neglected in your parenting, thus making you feel more guilty—not less! Remember, the starting line is today, and the goal is not perfection but faithfulness. Stay rooted in God's blueprint for parenting, and guilt, fear and doubt will not plague you.

The layout of this chapter is different from the others. Each of the seven principles is discussed, followed by ideas of how to implement them in the daily life of motherhood. This chapter is not meant to be read in one sitting. Doing so would be like eating a seven-course meal too quickly. None of the meal would be adequately savored nor digested, because there is just too much. Take one or two principles at a time, and give yourself a chance to digest them. In studying these seven traits, you are likely to evaluate your own maturity in each area; I know I did. Before becoming teachers of wisdom, we must first become students.

PRODUCTIVITY

*"Lazy hands make a man poor, but
diligent hands bring wealth."*

(Prov. 10:4—5)

*"Do not love sleep or you will grow poor;
stay awake and you will have food to spare."*

(Prov. 20:13—14)

The diligence and discipline to work hard is an invaluable gift
to give our children. In times past, most kids learned the value of
hard work by necessity. Take my grandfather, for example. He was
the youngest of fifteen children. (This was before washing
machines, disposable diapers, television, dishwashers and vacuum
cleaners. I think it was also before birth control!) His father's
wages as a produce vendor were insufficient to feed the family.
Every child worked hard. The oldest ones sold fruit and vegetables
with their father. Girls were in charge of cleaning, cooking and
watching the little children. Everyone was up before the crack of
dawn and worked until bedtime. Nothing was wasted, and leisure
was a rarity. The goal was survival. My grandfather started driving

tractors and trucks before he was ten. As an adult, he began work every day at 4:00 A.M. and worked hard without complaint. Diligence and prudence were bred into his character.

You might say that my grandfather's circumstances were an extreme exception. But are they? It's more likely that *we* are the exception. Far more people in the world live in poverty than in wealth. We live in an unusual time and in a very wealthy nation.

I am so glad that my children have more than enough nutritious food to eat, access to medical care, a bed to sleep in and the opportunity to learn and enjoy life. But I am also aware of the dangers of comfort. Although wealth and provisions are blessings, they can interfere with character development. The greatest warning about wealth comes not from Proverbs but from Jesus. He explained that riches can keep us from seeking and depending upon God (Matt. 6:19–21, 24; 19:23–24).

Giving our children the things that they desire is so tempting. We don't want to see them struggle or go without good things. Why should they miss out on parties, sporting events and good times because they are busy working? We don't want them to have to wear hand-me-downs when their friends are sporting the latest designer wear. However, in our quest to provide well for our kids, we may rob them of what brings lasting satisfaction. Research has consistently shown that children who have significant household responsibilities are better adjusted as adults than those children who did not have jobs. Learning to work hard at a young age not only predicts financial and job success in adulthood, but also healthier marriages and relationships!

The sixteen-year-old who gets a BMW for her birthday and spends her summers at the country club may be the envy of all of her peers. However, her parents have done her no favors in the long run. Experts in the field of leadership development warn wealthy parents to pass on their work ethic rather than lavishing children with excesses. Use your wealth (whether it is substantial or modest) to build character in your children. When children are given every advantage in life, they can become demanding,

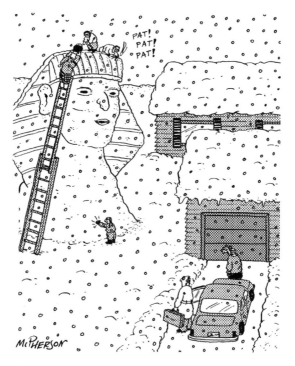

"Amazing how industrious they can be when the Nintendo is broken, isn't it?"

Reprinted by permission of John McPherson, as appeared in Chicken Soup for the Soul Cartoons *for Moms.*

lazy, ungrateful and spendthrift. However, kids that have significant chores and responsibilities learn time management, discipline, humility and the value of money. They also gain confidence as they become valued contributors to the family and society.

Ideas for Teaching Productivity

WORK

The most obvious way to teach a child to work hard is to give him work. Household chores, schoolwork and eventually outside jobs need to be a normal part of a child's daily life. Although this concept isn't exactly rocket science, surprisingly few homes implement it. At least initially, it takes time to give your children responsibilities. What mother doesn't tire of reminding her children of chores and checking to make sure they are done correctly? The clothes are folded much more neatly if you do it yourself!

Children as young as three can begin doing jobs that contribute to the functioning of the home. Not only do jobs teach responsibility, but they communicate to a child that she is a necessary part of the family. As children grow, their responsibilities should expand. Gauging how much responsibility is appropriate for children of different ages is sometimes difficult. Here are some suggestions:

Three to four years old: Set the napkins on the table for meals, put away toys.

Five to six years old: Set and clear the table, empty trash cans, make bed, dress self in morning, dusting.

Seven to nine years old: Fold clothes, wash dishes, feed and clean up after pets, vacuum, wash windows.

Ten to thirteen years old: (Along with any of the above) caring for younger siblings (not infants) while parents are still in the house, help with cooking and laundry, take out trash, cleaning.

In addition to household chores, most kids are ready to begin outside jobs starting at around age thirteen or fourteen. They can start with paper routes, mowing lawns, washing cars, shining shoes or baby-sitting.

If you can afford it, a great alternative to a summer job is volunteer work. For example, a fifteen-year-old can work at a church or other charity for the summer and earn a supplemental income from his parents. Jobs in nonprofit organizations such as churches, crisis pregnancy centers, soup kitchens, retirement homes, summer camps and animal shelters provide tremendous opportunities for character-building and discovering future career interests.

Although kids have to say no to some other activities, work builds lasting character and teaches invaluable life lessons. Youth is fleeting, and we should encourage our kids to enjoy their childhood. However, fun needs to be balanced with appropriate responsibility.

EARN AND MANAGE THEIR OWN MONEY

"What's for dinner?" Michael asked one evening.

"We are having the leftover chicken from last night," I replied.

"Not again!" Michael and Andrew said in unison. "Why can't we order pizza?"

"Because pizza costs money," I explained.

"I'll pay for it," Michael volunteered. He and Andrew ran upstairs and shook all of the change out of their piggy banks. "Look, we have twelve dollars!" Michael reported.

"You could buy a pizza for twelve dollars, but that is all the money you have earned doing chores for a long time. If you spend it on pizza, it will be all gone. You won't have any money to buy presents for people on their birthdays or to buy something you want later," I explained. Suddenly, leftover chicken didn't look so bad.

Teaching kids the value of money is a key part of productivity. They need to learn that money is a limited commodity and that it is directly related to work. Most teenagers have no concept of how much their clothes, cars, stereos and food actually cost. Money has no more value than dollars from a Monopoly game. If you run out, Mom and Dad always have more.

As a financial planner, my father was way ahead of his time when it came to teaching us about money. He implemented parenting strategies that experts are now suggesting. We started earning small allowances at age five if we completed all of our chores. The older we grew, both our responsibilities and our compensation increased.

On my thirteenth birthday, my dad took me to the bank to open up a checking account. He taught me how to write checks and balance the checkbook. At thirteen, I also began to get my clothing allowance. Every month I received fifty dollars in addition to my regular allowance. I could spend the money on whatever I wanted, after a 10 percent tithe, but I was responsible for buying all of my own clothes. If I wanted to go see a movie with friends, buy Christmas presents or wear designer shoes, it came out of my own money.

Creative parents take this a step further. One father I know has a "Bank of Daddy." When his children save their money, they earn 30 percent interest so they learn the advantage of saving. Parents can teach older kids financial lessons by cosigning a credit card (with a small limit) that the child *must* pay off every month. Other parents buy their children small shares of stock for birthday gifts to teach about investments.

The amount of personal debt in our culture is astounding. How few among us are good stewards of financial resources! Young adults who know how to earn, save and manage money have a tremendous advantage over those who do not.

Don't make privileges a given

One of the greatest pitfalls of our current parenting culture is confusing needs with privileges. In many homes, kids assume they are *entitled* to television, video games, athletic gear, telephones, elaborate vacations, computers, toys, camp, overnight sleepovers, extravagant birthday parties and stereo systems. These items and events should be luxuries and privileges, not entitlements. Parents often think about suspending one of these luxuries when a child misbehaves. For example, Justin comes home with a bad report card, so his parents take away his Sony PlayStation for a month. Sounds reasonable, right? The problem is a subtle psychological message. Justin had the PlayStation and assumes it as a given. His parents are the bad guys by taking away what is rightfully his. A healthier approach is to communicate from day one that the PlayStation is a *privilege to be earned,* not a right to be revoked.

By being productive and responsible, a child may earn the privilege to watch television, have a phone in her room, go over to a friend's house for the weekend or play on the volleyball team. These privileges can be revoked at any time if not managed responsibly. The child has the choice to earn or lose the privilege.

FIND OPPORTUNITIES TO SERVE

Another angle of productivity is prudence and discretion with what God has given us. Productivity for the sake of amassing wealth and comfort is not biblical. We are called to invest our time and abilities and then to use the fruits of our work for God's purposes. Scripture is filled with reminders to be generous to the needy. A life without hunger and poverty can leave us selfish and impervious to the suffering of others. Understanding the plight of a single mom living paycheck to paycheck is difficult, unless you've been there. Even further removed is the suffering of people worldwide. How will our children learn to be compassionate and giving when they have never known poverty? Short-term mission trips, volunteering at local charities, sponsoring a child or giving money to someone in need are all family activities that can teach children that productivity must by governed by compassion.

Proverbs addressing productivity: 6:6–11; 10:4–5, 26; 12:11, 14, 24, 27; 13:4, 11; 14:23; 15:9; 17:18; 19:15, 17, 24; 20:4, 13, 16; 21:5, 17, 20, 25–26; 22:9, 13, 16, 26; 24:30–34; 26:13–16; 28:19

Productivity

1. How do you teach your children the value of productivity?

_____

_____

2. Are there privileges that your children have begun to expect as rights? How might reframing these privileges help teach productivity?

_____

_____

UNCOMPROMISING INTEGRITY

The integrity of the upright guides them,
but the unfaithful are destroyed
by their duplicity.

(Prov. 11:3)

Better a little with righteousness than
much gain with injustice.

(Prov. 16:8)

George O'Leary had two loves in his life: football and the University of Notre Dame. Imagine his joy when his dream of coaching the Fighting Irish was realized! Five days after he was hired as Notre Dame's head football coach, O'Leary resigned his dream job and a lucrative salary. Why?

"Many years ago, as a young married father, I sought to pursue my dream as a football coach," he said. "In seeking employment I prepared a resume that contained inaccuracies regarding my completion of course work for a master's degree and also my level of participation in football at my alma mater. These misstatements were never stricken from my resume or biographical sketch in later years."

In his zeal to achieve his dream, George O'Leary cut a corner. He stretched the truth about his education and football experience in order to secure a head coaching job as a young man. As he aged and progressed, the lie followed him. He couldn't change his resume without admitting his dishonesty. Years later, his success as a head coach won him the coveted job at Notre Dame. A lie told twenty years earlier to catapult his career eventually destroyed his dream and sterling reputation.

The headlines often provide examples of hardworking, intelligent people who get caught cutting corners. They are living reminders of the wisdom in Proverbs 21:5–6: "The plans of the diligent lead to profit as surely as haste leads to poverty. A fortune made by a lying tongue is a fleeting vapor and a deadly snare." Productivity without integrity eventually destroys you!

In the race to get good grades, win the soccer match, earn extra money, win a scholarship or get accepted by a prestigious college, kids are tempted to take shortcuts. Even God-fearing parents may justify their children's subtle dishonesty: "Everyone does it. The other kids have an unfair advantage!" But Proverbs tells us there is no eternal advantage to dishonesty.

Every two years, the Joseph and Edna Josephson Foundation conducts a major study of American teens. *Report Card 2002: The Ethics of American Youth* proved how few teenagers value their integrity. In a survey of twelve-thousand teenagers, here are the percentages that reported engaging in the following unethical behaviors in the prior year:

93 percent lied to their parents

86 percent lied to teachers

74 percent cheated on a test

39 percent said they would lie in order to get a better job

38 percent engaged in theft

The study also found little difference in results based on public versus private schooling or religious affiliation. If parents do not teach their children character, they certainly will not learn it anywhere else!

Ideas for **Teaching Integrity**

Redefine Success

Lying, cheating and stealing are so attractive because they often lead to success. Many times, nice guys do finish last. Unlike George O'Leary, most people tell occasional lies without getting caught. Kids who cheat on tests may receive better grades than those who walk the straight and narrow. Inevitably, your kids will ask the question that David asked repeatedly, "Why do the bad guys win?"

If success is simply winning the race, those without integrity may succeed. However, God is looking for "a few good men" (and women) who define success as honoring Him. "For the eyes of the LORD range throughout the earth to strengthen those whose hearts are fully committed to Him" (2 Chron. 16:9).

Ultimately God will exalt whomever He wants. Wealth and status do not define success. Whether rich or poor, educated or not, servant or leader, a success is someone who walks with integrity, trusting God for the result.

> Whether rich or poor, educated or not, servant or leader, a success is someone who walks with integrity, trusting God for the result.

Repeatedly, we must define success for our children according to God's standards. If you see your kid cheating or showing poor sportsmanship on the playing field, yank them off. If they play hard but show kindness and integrity, reward them. Resist praising them only for the results (wins, grades, awards) but foremost for their character through the process.

NEVER TOLERATE DISHONESTY

"The lamp in the living room is broken. Which one of you did it?"

Most parents wouldn't be surprised to hear flat denials from their children in this situation. What kid doesn't, at some point, try to escape culpability with a little lie? In the long run, does it really matter who broke the vase?

Lying often seems as natural to children as running. "Daddy, can I have some candy?" "What did Mommy say?" "She said it was okay."

A lie is a lie is a lie. Today it might be cute and harmless. But letting little children get away with dishonesty sets a pattern that is difficult if not impossible to break later in life. As any parent of a teenager knows, trust is the lifeblood of a parent-child relationship. Trust is absolutely critical and must be taught throughout parenting, not just when lies become dangerous.

Proverb 12:22 says, "The Lord detests lying lips, but he delights in men who are truthful."

Kids should know that the worst thing they can do is to be dishonest. The punishment for breaking Mom's favorite vase should be nothing compared to the punishment for lying about it.

A GOOD NAME

A good name is more desirable than great riches; to be esteemed is better than silver or gold.

(Prov. 22:1)

If you live in a small town, you know the value of a good name. Everyone knows who is honest and who isn't. Those who enjoy a good name do anything to protect it. Do your children know they represent your name? A friend wrote this poem for Mike to give to our boys. It communicates the importance placed on their integrity.

A GOOD NAME

Dear child, as you grow older, so much I long to give,
No greater gift can I give you, than a life of honor lived.
I bore the name of Slattery, but with this honor, what would I do?
For as a child, it never occurred to me, I would pass my name to you.

But I chose wisely to protect it, to add integrity and weight.
This name became more special when I shared it with my mate.
When you came into our family, we shared our name with you.
A living demonstration of what is good and what is true.
Together we built a household. We built it out of love.
And when we needed answers, we looked to God above.
Our good name must be treasured, more than finest gold.
Good reputations can't be purchased, but too often they are sold.
They take a lifetime to establish, but can be lost in just a day,
But unlike fame and fortune, a good name is here to stay.
More valuable than riches, my good name I now impart,
This legacy I leave to you, my child, with all my heart.

Amy McDougald

You may not have grown up with the luxury of a good name. Perhaps your struggle has been to overcome your family name. Remember that whatever your family name may be, you also carry the name of "Christian." Christ has charged us with protecting and guarding the sterling name He imparted on the cross. How many people throughout history have rejected Christianity, not because of Christ but because of the immorality of Christians? More important than the reputations of our families is the name of our Savior. Let us carry it and teach our children to represent it with integrity.

A coach known previously for his integrity learned the difficult lesson that shortcutting character is dangerous. Upon resigning his position at Notre Dame, George O'Leary had this to say: "I pray that my experiences will simply be yet another coaching lesson to the youth of this country that we are all accountable for our actions and there can be no double standard."

Proverbs that address integrity: 10:9; 11:1, 3–6, 20, 29; 12:13, 19, 22; 13:5, 25; 15:27–28; 16:8, 11; 19:1, 5, 22; 20:7; 21:5–6; 22:1; 24:12; 25:26; 28:6, 20

Uncompromising Integrity

1. How can you appropriately define success for your children?

_____

_____

2. Why is a "good name" important? How did the character of your family name affect you growing up? How can you teach your children the value of building and maintaining a good name?

_____

_____

RESTRAINED SPEECH

A man of knowledge uses words with restraint,
and a man of understanding is even-tempered.
Even a fool is thought wise if he keeps silent,
and discerning if he holds his tongue.

(Prov. 17:27–28)

The tongue has the power of life and death,
and those who love it will eat its fruits.

(Prov. 18:21)

When words are many, sin is not absent,
but he who holds his tongue is wise.

(Prov. 10:19)

One refreshing aspect of young children is that they blurt out exactly what they are thinking. This trait leads to some of the funniest and also most embarrassing experiences of motherhood. Kids have no qualms about asking someone why they have no hair on their head or sharing that "Mommy says you have bad taste. What does 'bad taste' mean?" My son Andrew has an incredible sense of smell, which he readily displays whenever we visit a public restroom. "It smells like pooh-pooh in here!" He announces. "Is that lady under there making pooh-pooh? She's stinky! I'm only going to make pee-pee so I won't stink!"

Along with the cute and embarrassing comments also come hurtful, sassy, foul, complaining, defiant and deceitful words. Who could guess such vile things would originate from the mouths of our dear, sweet children? Much of a parent's discipline revolves around teaching children what to say and not to say.

To make our job more difficult, most of us struggle with restraining our own tongues. Five minutes after scolding your child for losing her temper, you fly off the handle at your husband. James tells us that anyone who can perfectly control their tongue has achieved perfection in all areas. I, for one, know how far I am from such perfection! As James wrote, the tongue is both destructive and impossible to tame perfectly:

> When we put bits into the mouths of horses to make them obey us, we can turn the whole animal. Or take ships as an example. Although they are so large and are driven by strong winds, they are steered by a very small rudder wherever the pilot wants to go. Likewise the tongue is a small part of the body, but it makes great boasts. Consider what a great forest is set on fire by a small spark. The tongue also is a fire, a world of evil among the parts of the body. It corrupts the whole person, sets the whole course of his life on fire, and is itself set on fire by hell.
>
> (Jas. 3:3–6)

Lies, gossip, cursing, cutting remarks, flattery, sharing secrets, careless prattle . . . all ways that a tongue can destroy relationships and lives. How many times I have wished to lasso my words back into my mouth after seeing the damage they have caused others! James is right. Taming the tongue is a colossal endeavor.

James continues his discourse on the tongue by commenting on how fickle it is: "With the tongue we praise our Lord and Father, and with it we curse men, who have been made in God's likeness. Out of the same mouth come praise and cursing. My brothers, this should not be" (Jas. 3:9–10).

How true are James's words! Try as I might to say the right things, foul and destructive words find their way through my lips. The tongue ultimately reveals what is in our hearts. Battling the tongue is a discipline not rooted merely in restraining our speech. Sooner or later, it leads to examining our hearts. Your attention to training your child's tongue may focus on the words that are said but eventually such training impacts thoughts and attitudes.

Ideas for Teaching Restrained Speech

Set high standards of what can be said at home

No swearing is an obvious rule for most Christian homes. But other destructive speech can easily slip under the radar, compromising family relationships. Siblings (and parents and spouses) can be scathingly critical of each other. Often cruel words are couched in teasing, making them seem less malicious. Kids are inevitably going to run up against cutting comments at school and in the neighborhood. Home should be a haven where they feel supported and loved.

"But teasing and fighting are just normal parts of family life," you might say. Kids naturally fall into criticizing each other. However, normal and acceptable are two different things. Lying is also normal for kids! Parents have the authority to set and enforce standards for what is said at home.

Parent-child and sibling relationships become a child's blueprint for all of their relationships. Fighting fairly, dealing with anger, asking for forgiveness, seasoning speech with sensitivity, demonstrating respect for authority, showing kindness—all these lessons are or are not learned through the way tongues are used at home. Given that the homestead is where emotions often run the highest, restraining speech with family members is easier said than done. Like any discipline, it requires a consistent commitment to teaching and enforcing clearly defined limits of permissible speech.

SET THE EXAMPLE

Children, by and large, learn what is acceptable speech based on what their parents say. Those little ears are always listening when we talk to our husbands, talk on the phone, yell at people in traffic, share a juicy piece of gossip. . . . Scolding our children for swearing has little impact when we later demonstrate our own grasp of forbidden words!

Although we strive to perfectly tame our tongues, we are going to slip up. Fortunately, children can learn not only from our successes but also from the way we handle our mistakes.

Let's say you have been teaching your preteen daughter about the dangers of gossip. Then one day she overhears you talking about the neighbors' marital spats. Your natural response is to be defensive—to explain that you were not gossiping, you were just "sharing a concern." Instead, admit that you were not being careful about what you said. It's okay for our kids to know that this is something that grown-ups continually work on too.

HELP KIDS LEARN THE CONSEQUENCES OF DESTRUCTIVE SPEECH

Ask any child, "What is worse? Hitting your brother, or saying mean things to him?" Most likely, their response will be that hitting is worse. The damage of a punch is visible and measurable. Kids that wouldn't think of physically hurting someone else might flippantly use critical and malicious words.

Words are destructive.

Although speech is intangible, its consequences often are not. Let your children feel the damage their words can cause. When your daughter mouths off, she loses privileges. Your son and his friend gang up on a younger sibling all day, teasing and taunting. Guess what? No more friends until your son can learn to treat his sister kindly. No child completely escapes feeling the pain of others' words, yet they so readily hurt with their own tongues. Remind your children of what it felt like when they were on the receiving end of unkind words.

Replace the old adage, "Sticks and stones may break my bones, but words will never hurt me," with a proverb from the Word of God: "Like a club or a sword or a sharp arrow is the man who gives false testimony against his neighbor" (Prov. 25:18).

GIVE INSTRUCTIONS OF WHAT *TO* SAY

Don't swear, don't lie, don't sass, don't complain, don't gossip, don't yell, don't tease. A roll of masking tape should do the trick! Part of avoiding destructive talk is learning how to engage in affirmative speech. A child can more easily refrain from the negative if you give them something positive to say. "I know you are mad. You cannot say, 'I hate my sister,' but you can tell me why you are angry." Perhaps God tells us to pray for our enemies for this reason: to keep our tongues too busy to curse them!

Play games that teach your kids to compliment others, to ask good questions, and to listen and stay silent for a time. "I want each of you to ask Sarah three questions so you can learn more about her." "Let's see who can be quiet for five minutes" (my personal favorite). "It's Amy's birthday. Go around the table and share what you love about Amy."

Tongues are not all bad. Along with Solomon's warnings about a fool's flippant tongue are proverbs proclaiming how healing and refreshing encouraging words can be. "Reckless words pierce like a sword, but the tongue of the wise brings healing" (Prov. 12:18).

My heart fills with joy when encouraging and kind words spontaneously come from my children. Hearing them use their tongues constructively is so exciting. How God's heart must be delighted when His children use the gift of speech to build each other up and to offer words of praise and thanksgiving!

Proverbs that address restrained speech: 4:24; 10:19–21, 31–32; 11:9, 12–13; 12:5-6, 13–14, 18, 23; 13:3; 14:3; 15:2, 28; 16:23; 17:7–9, 19, 27–28; 18:7, 20–21; 21:23; 25:18, 23; 26:18–22, 28; 29:20

Restrained Speech

1. Why is restraining your tongue so difficult?

_____

_____

2. How do you see your children failing to restrain their speech?

_____

_____

3. Ephesians 4 suggests that changes in our speech result from spiritual renewal through our dependence on Christ. How are you seeking this renewal in your life? How can you encourage it in your children?

_____

_____

POSITIVE RELATIONSHIPS

He who walks with the wise grows wise,
but a companion of fools
suffers harm.

(Prov. 13:20)

Do not make friends with a
hot-tempered man, do not associate
with one easily angered.

(Prov. 22:24)

As iron sharpens iron,
so one man sharpens another.

(Prov. 27:17)

Friends are an important factor in every stage of life. Children as young as two or three begin to enjoy playing with other kids. Preschool and school-aged children quickly make and lose friends, learning lessons about relationships along the way. However, the influence of friends takes on a whole new meaning as children approach adolescence.

Go to a mall or high school football game, and observe the group behavior of kids between the ages of twelve and eighteen.

You can tell who belongs with which group. They dress the same, talk the same and act the same. If you have adolescents at home, you know firsthand how influential peers become. Your kid may seem like she's changing identities overnight based on her group of associates.

Parents of teens have valid concerns about their kids' friends. Problems with drugs, sex, disrespect, smoking, foul language and rotten attitudes often originate from negative peers. As 1 Corinthians 15:33 says, "Bad company corrupts good morals." Some parents address this problem by severely limiting their children's contact with the "outside world." Unfortunately, this strategy often results in children who are painfully timid or who become rebellious when given a taste of freedom.

Identifying with a peer group is a normal and necessary stage of adolescent development, helping kids practice who they want to become apart from their parents. As adolescents begin the task of separating from their family, they feel incredibly insecure. Being part of a group or clique provides a transitional identity. Fortunately, the group thinking of adolescents is replaced by the independence of young adulthood. However, some of the attitudes and behaviors that adolescents encourage in each other do irreparable damage. The goal of steering teens toward safe peer groups begins with laying the right foundation in childhood.

Ideas for Encouraging Positive Peer Groups

CHOOSE ACTIVITIES WITH PEERS IN MIND

Your children make friends where they spend time. If you want them to develop a peer group with positive values, they have to spend time where those kids do. Religious schools, churches or organizations are by no means safe havens. Even in the most innocent settings, kids can find ways to create mischief. However, families that teach character are more likely to be involved in activities and organizations that reinforce similar values. Particularly in the preteen and teen years, make an effort to keep your kids busy in healthy, positive activities.

You may also need to steer your children away from places with particularly bad influences. Brian is a great soccer player and was offered the opportunity to play on a traveling team. Because of his exceptional ability, Brian is the youngest player on the team. As his parents observe the team, they notice that the coach encourages rough play. He uses coarse language and yells at the kids often. Also, many of the strong players on the team are disrespectful and sarcastic. Only two weeks into the season, his parents noticed a change in Brian's behavior and attitudes. Although playing on the soccer team is a wonderful opportunity, is the influence of a negative peer group too high a price to pay?

MAKE YOUR HOUSE KID-FRIENDLY

What mom wants her house littered with toys and games, blaring with loud music, and regularly trampled by five or six kids? Life is a lot calmer when the kids all play at someone else's house! However, there is no better way to subtly keep tabs on your kids and their friends than for your house to be home base. Some parents put in pools and build game rooms for this very reason.

Lori and Jim Taylor made a concerted effort to become the house on the block where kids were always welcome. Cast parties, sleepovers, movie night, Bible studies, and pick up games all happened at the Taylor's. Their backyard was littered with footballs, soccer goals, an obstacle course and a trampoline. Their basement had a dart board, fooseball table, and the latest video game system. Lori's kitchen was always stocked with snacks to feed her four children and all the friends who might wander through. Although there were many areas of her house that were off-limits to kids, everyone felt welcomed. "You're nuts!" her friends often told her. "You might as well be the church youth leader!"

There were days that Lori and Jim wished that another parent would volunteer their house as the designated hangout. But more often, they became convinced of the value of ministering to their own children and so many others through their hospitality. Countless afternoons, kids sat at the kitchen counter and shared their thoughts and concerns over a sandwich and lemonade. These parents truly understood the people and pressures in their children's lives.

Having a kid-friendly house does not mean that you have to be overly involved. Some mothers go to the extreme, dressing and talking like their child's peer group. Kids need some freedom; they also need you to remain in an adult role. You can monitor what is going on without abdicating your mom-status. Although you may host a sleepover for your daughter's thirteen-year-old friends, thankfully you don't have to eat pizza with them and bunk up in a sleeping bag. Kids whose parents are intrusive (as opposed to involved) can become resentful and secretive.

TEACH YOUR CHILDREN TO *CHOOSE* GOOD FRIENDS

Learning to discern who is a good friend takes time. A parent's job is not to choose friends for her children, but to teach her kids how to make good choices themselves. At a young age, kids can learn qualities of good friends. They can also learn the painful lessons from someone who is not to be trusted.

"It seems like every time Jill is over, you guys fight a lot." "I noticed that your feelings seem to get hurt often when you spend time with Kurt." "How

> A parent's job is not to choose friends for her children, but to teach her kids how to make good choices themselves.

do you feel when you are over at Jason's house?" "The last three times you went out with that group, you got into trouble." "What qualities do you like about Kate?" These types of questions and observations teach kids to evaluate their peer group.

Positive comments and encouraging feedback should be common as well. Compliment your children when they choose quality friends. Encourage them when they reach out to less popular children or stand up to peer pressure. Sometimes we can be so paranoid about the bad choices they may make that we take the good choices for granted.

Your kids may pick some friends that you don't like, for one reason or another. While some might be annoying or inconsiderate, others may be downright destructive. Discerning the difference is important. Keep in mind that kids identify with peers. If you reject their friends, they feel like you are rejecting them. You need to have valid, behavioral reasons that spending time with a particular individual or group is unwise (even if you choose not to specifically share these reasons). Let's face it: Most preteens and teenagers (including our own) can be insensitive, immature and goofy, and your kids need to hang out with *someone!* Fortunately, the majority of adolescent relationships are short-lived, but the lessons kids learn along the way make a lifelong impact. Peer groups are an unavoidable part of your children's development. Pray that God brings good friends into the lives of your children.

TEACH YOUR CHILD TO *BECOME* A GOOD FRIEND

Just as your children are seeking kind, loyal friends, other children who want good friends are seeking those qualities. To have your children look for good friends is not enough. They must also learn how to become a good friend to others.

None of us were born with the milk of human kindness pouring out of us. We all began wanting life on our own terms. Remember what play group was like with a group of toddlers? The moms play referee as the children bite each other and fight over toys. Kids need to *learn* what being a good friend means. At very young ages, learning to share and not cause bodily harm is the goal. As kids grow, so does their potential to harm each other. Cliques, teasing, gossip, breaking confidences and jealousy become the weapons of choice.

Your children experience both the giving and receiving end of hurt as they develop social maturity. They endure arguments, betrayals and rejection. You play an important role in helping them understand how to behave toward their friends. When your son has a fight with his best friend, do they work it out or write each other off? When your daughter's three good friends get together without her, how should she respond?

How we teach our children to interact with other people is a critical part of motherhood. John 13:35 says, "By this all men will know that you are my disciples, if you love one another." In other words, the primary evidence of our relationship with Christ is the character of our relationships. Practically the entire New Testament is devoted to teaching us how to love others and share Christ with them. Little that we can teach our children is more important than showing them how to relate well to others. Isn't this largely how Jesus spent his time with his apostles— teaching about relationships?

Manners, respect for others, appropriate assertiveness, self-control, kindness, sensitivity and obedience to authority all represent how moms teach their children to relate. And boy, do we have a lot of opportunities to do this teaching! Not a day goes by that a mother isn't involved in the relationships of her children. She negotiates fights between siblings and sets the rules for engagement. She decides (or at least tries to decide) which friends her children can spend time with. She helps her teenager navigate through the quagmires of dating and social cliques. Perhaps her most profound contribution is her own modeling of relationships. How does she handle conflict? How does she respond to a friend in need? Does she gossip or slander others? Does she show love to those who are undeserving of love, including wayward and rebellious children? Does she set healthy boundaries with others, or does she give into bullying and manipulation? How does she respond to her husband?

Social discipleship is a large aspect of motherhood. Your children emerge with distinct ideas and patterns of interacting largely based on your conscious and subtle teaching over the years.

Proverbs that address peers: 1:10–15; 2:12–20; 3:3, 27–30; 4:14–17; 10:12; 11:16–17; 13:20; 20:19; 22:24; 23:19–21; 24:1–2; 27:10, 17; 28:7

Positive Relationships

1. Reflect on some of the friends you had as a child/adolescent. How did your friends impact you?

   _____

   _____

2. How did your parents' attitudes and behaviors impact your choice of friends?

   _____

   _____

3. How do you feel about the friends your children are choosing?

   _____

   _____

4. How do you feel about the friends your children are becoming?

   _____

   _____

OPENNESS TO FEEDBACK

Whoever corrects a mocker invites insult;
whoever rebukes a wicked man incurs abuse.
Do not rebuke a mocker or he will hate you; rebuke a
wise man and he will love you. Instruct a wise man
and he will be wiser still; teach a righteous man
and he will add to his learning.

(Prov. 9:7–9)

He who ignores discipline comes to poverty and shame,
but whoever heeds correction is honored.

(Prov. 13:18)

A man who remains stiff-necked after many rebukes
will suddenly be destroyed–without remedy.

(Prov. 29:1)

Perhaps nothing distinguishes the wise from the foolish more than their response to constructive feedback. The ability to learn from even painful instruction is a hallmark of maturity. Wise people are not only open to feedback, but they actively seek instruction.

Have you ever asked someone for feedback only to hear them say, "Do you really want to know?" *Do* you really want to know? Are you ready and willing to hear the truth even if it is painful? Or would you rather pretend that the bad does not exist? Although we may extol the great benefits of accountability, most of us hate to be called on our weaknesses. Accountability is great as long as it doesn't hit too close to home!

As a psychologist, I meet with people who for one reason or another are seeking change. However, many are not willing to make significant change or to accept painful feedback about their own part in a problem. We always do things for a reason. Most of us prefer to feel victimized by these reasons rather than to embrace accountability for our own behavior. We would rather stay stuck than admit a weakness like anger, selfish motives or laziness.

Claire came to counseling because of the dismal state of her marriage. She described her husband, Joe, as "emotionally dead." According to Claire, Joe worked ten hours a day, came home and flopped into his easy chair until bedtime. When I asked Claire if Joe would come to counseling, she adamantly stated that she didn't want him there. I met with Claire for a handful of sessions, giving her time to express her loneliness and frustration. Then I began challenging her to move towards forgiveness. I suggested that she may be contributing to her loneliness, pushing Joe away with her anger and bitterness. That was the last time I saw Claire. She was only willing to meet with me as long as I was affirming of her victim role.

Growth is impossible without being open to feedback. Maturity and wisdom can develop only when we accept and integrate instruction. Ask any teacher which she would rather have: a brilliant student who has no interest in learning or an average student with an insatiable appetite for knowledge? Wisdom is wasted on a person who stubbornly refuses correction. Both resistance and openness to feedback begin in childhood. A coachable spirit is an invaluable trait to encourage in children.

Ideas for Teaching Openness to Feedback

CORRECT YOUR CHILD WITH LOVE

"But I don't want to hurt her feelings!" Some parents are so concerned about their children feeling loved that they shy away from correcting them. They may even be defensive when others say negative things about their children. Teachers know the frustration of meeting with a protective parent to discuss "Johnny's behavior" only to have the blame placed on "poor classroom management."

Children largely form their self-concept from the relationship they have with their parents. Children who are continually praised and not confronted never accept their own limitations. Loving children through their limitations is a vital aspect of building self-confidence. Children who have not received loving correction never integrate their own weaknesses and continually feel the need to project perfection. As adults, they become defensive and desperate to hide their limitations from others.

> Children who have not received loving correction never integrate their own weaknesses and continually feel the need to project perfection.

Feedback can be scary. Being confronted with our faults can awaken deep fears of rejection. This is particularly true of children, because a child's thinking is very black and white. When he is being praised, he feels loved and cherished. When he is punished, he can feel unlovable and worthless. Children learn to defend against correction largely because they associate doing wrong with parental rejection—their greatest fear. Most children who have suffered losses (divorce, death or abandonment) believe their own misbehavior caused the parent to leave.

For these reasons, correction must always be done within the safe confines of a loving, trusting relationship. A child's disobedience should temporarily change the tone of a parent-child interaction. However, it should never threaten to sever the bond.

I remember counseling a ten-year-old boy who was in foster care. The boy's father abandoned him shortly after his birth. His mother died when the child was only three. He had been in the same foster home since that time. His foster mother was a loving, caring woman. However, she often confronted his misbehavior by threatening to send him to an orphanage. The more she threatened, the worse his behavior became. The boy constantly pushed the envelope to see how far he could go before he would yet again be abandoned. His incredible anxiety of being rejected drove his behavior.

Although encouragement and affection are always important, communicating them is essential when a child is corrected. A confrontation should always be sandwiched between loving and affirming words. Expressing disappointment with a child is fine, but never threaten to withhold love. Assuring them of your unconditional love allows them the security to accept constructive feedback.

Have you ever had the experience of being loved in the face of great shame? In the counseling room, people sometimes share secrets for the first time in their lives. A fifty-year-old woman reveals that she had an abortion thirty years ago. A middle-aged man confides that he was sexually abused by his grandfather. Such secrets have been locked away for years because of the fear of rejection. Love in the face of our open sin and shame is the most powerful medicine on earth.

God models this dynamic in His relationship with His children. He tells us that nothing can separate us from His love. Although He disciplines us in truth, His love never changes. In fact, His correction is rooted in His love for us.

Proverbs 5:12 says, "the Lord disciplines those he loves, as a father the son he delights in."

Avoid making comparisons

If you have two or more children, you naturally compare them with each other. You notice that one is taller, learned to read faster, is more sensitive or looks more like you than the other. Noticing the differences between children is not only unavoidable but imperative to good parenting. Kids are all different and need to be parented differently.

Noticing differences and using them to motivate behavior are two separate matters. When eight-year-old Holly is sitting quietly at the restaurant while five-year-old brother Sam is jumping on the table, the comparison screams to be made. This trap is a tempting one to fall into. However, comparing children is ultimately a destructive way to give feedback about behavior.

Comparisons increase the competitive nature of siblings. Most siblings don't need any encouragement to be competitive. They naturally vie for the parents' attention and approval. Rare is the home in which brothers and sisters have not debated who is Mom and Dad's favorite. Even Jesus' disciples argued about who among them would be the greatest (Matt. 18:1). In this competitive spirit, siblings become opponents to be beaten rather than teammates to be supported.

Comparisons also teach children to measure their behavior by the standards of others rather than by God's standards. Who cares what other kids are doing? Children all have different abilities and personalities. The standard should never be who received the better grades or who was better behaved, but what each has done with his own abilities. The Parable of the Talents is a great model for this (Matt. 25:14–28). The three characters in this parable were given ten, five, and one talent, respectively. Each was evaluated by what they individually did with what they had been given. Using comparisons with anyone is a dangerous way of giving feedback. Each of us has our own, unique pilgrimage. Looking at others eventually makes us feel either arrogant or inadequate. Life is not a contest to be won, but an offering to be given. Children should learn to strive to do their best, regardless of how they stack up to others.

MAKE FEEDBACK SPECIFIC AND BEHAVIORAL

Often when we correct our kids, we lead with the first words that come to mind. "All this noise is driving me crazy! Keep it down!" "Don't tell me you forgot your homework again. When will you learn to be more responsible?" Whether or not our feedback is constructive depends upon carefully choosing the right words. Great feedback is always both specific and behavioral.

Specific feedback pinpoints a specific action rather than an all-encompassing character trait. "You're not a very good friend to your sister" or "You're being lazy" seem like generalized judgments rather than instructive complaints. Instead, make very specific observations like: "Your room has not been cleaned in a week," "Please stop teasing Ashley," or "You have not completed your homework." These comments identify one explicit thing that the child is capable of addressing.

Helpful feedback is also behavioral. "Change your attitude!" is a good example of feedback that is too intangible. Attitudes are not behaviors; they are displayed by behavior. Whether or not a child is no longer lazy or works on being kinder are subjective. Behavioral feedback makes change very obvious. Even when addressing an attitude problem, make the required change very concrete. "You need to stop complaining." "Do not slam your bedroom door." "Don't roll your eyes when I ask you to do something. It is very disrespectful." "Your homework needs to be completed before 8:00."

Constructive correction, even when critical, empowers your children to improve rather than discouraging them from trying. The confidence to seek and accept constructive feedback is an invaluable tool that opens your child's heart to wisdom throughout their lifetime.

Proverbs that address openness to feedback: 9:7–9; 10:8, 17; 11:14; 12:1, 15; 13:1, 10, 13, 14, 18; 15:5, 22, 31–32; 16:20; 17:10; 18:15; 19:20, 25, 27; 20:5; 21:11; 23:9; 25:11–12; 27:5–6, 9; 28:14; 29:1

Openness to Feedback

1. What are some natural roadblocks your children may have to accepting and learning from feedback?

_____

2. How do you respond to constructive criticism? Why is it so difficult to accept?

_____

3. Think of a few areas in which each of your children need correction. Word this correction two ways: (1) addressing a trait (2) addressing a behavior. (For example, you are messy versus you need to clean your room.) What is the emotional difference between the two messages?

_____

SELF-CONTROL

Better a patient man than a warrior,
a man who controls his temper than
one who takes a city.

(Prov. 16:32)

Like a city whose walls are broken down
is a man who lacks self-control.

(Prov. 25:28)

Follow a toddler around for a day, and you get a taste of life without self-control. I think God made kids so cute between the ages of twelve and twenty-four months for a reason: If they weren't so cute, most parents would simply throw them out. Moms of toddlers can never rest at ease. Their conversations are constantly interrupted by "Don't touch that; no; don't hit Mommy; put the lipstick down; get your hands out of the toilet; we don't put ice cream in our hair. . . ." No matter the time, the setting or the circumstances, Junior is apt to find trouble. Toddlers grab whatever they see, yell when they have the urge, cry and scream if they don't get their way, bite, kick, hit, climb, rip, dump, paint and destroy. Apart from survival, most mothers' goal is to teach their children some small measure of self-control during these harried years.

The average child entering kindergarten has learned the basics of self-control. He is potty-trained, can get angry without throwing a tantrum, doesn't immediately blurt out everything that comes to mind and can sit still for at least a few minutes. These building blocks of self-discipline must continue to develop throughout childhood and adolescence.

Proverbs addresses the importance of self-control in three primary areas of functioning: anger, sexuality, and avoiding excesses. A lack of self-control in any of these three areas leads to disaster in adult lives. In fact, we can readily point to individuals whose lives have been ruined by uncontrolled rage, indiscriminate sexuality and overindulgence.

Anger

Christians often have a strange relationship with anger. We are not always sure if it is okay to be angry or not. Getting mad seems like a bad thing, but stuffing anger only makes matters worse. Although Scripture warns us of the danger of uncontrolled anger, being angry is *not* a sin. Psalm 4:4 says, "In your anger do not sin." Anger is a normal response to frustration and hurt. It can also be a defensive reaction to fear, jealousy, shame and sadness.

Anger that goes unrecognized and uncontrolled often leads to sin. A great example is found in the story of two brothers in

Genesis 4. When Cain was jealous of his brother Abel, read what God said to him: "Why are you angry? Why is your face downcast? If you do what is right, will you not be accepted? But if you do not do what is right, sin is crouching at your door; it desires to have you, but you must master it."

Some parents try to teach their children self-control in this area by denying and squelching anger. A thirteen-year-old is furious because his six-year-old sister colored on his school project. "She's

Mrs. Zanski's fifteen-minute slide presentation quickly set the tone for her parent-teacher conference with the Murdocks.

Reprinted by permission of John McPherson, as appeared in Chicken Soup for the Soul Cartoons for Moms.

just a little girl. She didn't know any better!" his parents coax. This boy's anger is a normal and understandable reaction to what happened. After all, Mom would be upset if the little girl destroyed a precious heirloom. Although his anger is natural, their son needs help learning how to express it appropriately.

Explosive anger is not the only problem parents need to look out for in their children. Some kids appear to have excellent self-control with their anger, only to be stuffing it or expressing it passively. Passive-aggressive behavior is a self-defeating form of venting anger. Kids often adopt this strategy when they feel overpowered by their parents. Instead of communicating their feelings of sadness or frustration, they pretend that nothing is wrong. They use subtle, passive behavior to express themselves. Some examples of passive aggression are being late, "forgetting" to complete tasks, laziness or sloppiness.

Neither explosive anger nor passive aggression is a healthy way of managing the natural feelings of anger. As a parent, you can help your children identify their anger, appropriately express it and address its causes.

Sexuality

In today's climate, few things cause parents more concern than the issue of sexuality. Morality has declined in every standard, but none more blatantly than in areas involving sexuality. Parents of seven-year-old girls are shocked by the provocative clothing designed for these innocents. Preadolescent boys are frequently exposed to pornography and explicit sexual conversation. Some studies indicate that over 80 percent of graduating high school seniors are sexually active. The stakes are high! Date rape, child sexual abuse, sexually transmitted diseases, teenage pregnancies and abortion are valid concerns for parents in this sexualized climate. Although not as apparent, the psychological and spiritual consequences of sexual misconduct are just as devastating as the physical.

A young couple beginning marriage faces some depressing odds. Marriage is difficult for anyone, but the baggage of pre-marital sexuality adds shame, low self-esteem, comparisons, resentment and distrust. Following God's standards for sexuality allows a couple to enter marriage with the confidence of God's favor. He rewards faithfulness. Yes, God is forgiving. A couple with a history of sexual misconduct is not doomed to unhappiness. However, the consequences of sin can be permanent. "Kids just being kids" rarely realize what they jeopardize by marginalizing God's standards for them.

Self-control in the area of sexuality is not just about saying no. More importantly, purity is rooted in not wanting to compromise God's plan for your life. Fortunately, some compelling and gifted young writers and speakers have developed resources that give young men and women a vision for purity. Tools for helping your children develop self-control in the area of sexuality include: *And the Bride Wore White,* by Dana Gresh; *Every Young Man's Battle,* by Stephen Aterburn; and *I Kissed Dating Good-bye* and *Not Even a Hint,* by Joshua Harris.

Avoiding Excess

Some areas of excess are clearly identified by most Christian parents. Drugs, alcohol and smoking are among them. However, other seemingly innocuous forms of excess can also destroy lives when left unchecked.

Gambling, shopping, eating, competition, amusement, losing weight, earning or saving money, neatness, collecting, watching television, and even working are all areas that can potentially lead to enslaving addictions. Although little concern is attached to titles like "shopaholic" or "workaholic," truly knowing the anguish that these excesses cause overshadows the innocent titles. In 1 Corinthians 6:12, Paul tells us, "'Everything is permissible for me'—but not everything is beneficial. 'Everything is permissible for me'—but I will not be mastered by anything." God has given our children much to enjoy, but the source of our pleasure can so easily become the cause of our pain when not governed by self-control.

Ideas for Teaching Self-Control

SETTING LIMITS

In each of the three critical areas of self-control, some limits are clear to everyone. Murder is not an acceptable expression of anger; fourteen-year-olds have no business having sex; snorting cocaine is an excessive form of pleasure. However, more subtle lines must be drawn to protect children from ever getting close to these gross violations. Where do you draw the limits? For example, some parents ban alcoholic beverages from their home while others allow their teenagers to have a glass of champagne on New Year's Eve. Can they both be right?

The worst thing a parent can do is to be paralyzed by indecision and draw no limits. Do your best to study Scripture, understand your child's strengths and weaknesses, and then enforce clear limits in all three of these danger areas. Young adolescents particularly can easily get in over their heads. They may not be able to tame their lust for sexual pleasure, peer acceptance or passionate aggression. Our job as parents is to set limits that keep our kids out of situations that are beyond their maturity. For example, a sixteen-year-old boy probably can't handle being in the house alone with his girlfriend.

TEACHING CONSEQUENCES

One common trait of childhood and adolescent thinking is the inability to project into the future. Teenagers also have a sense of immortality. They never believe that they can die driving recklessly or that they can get pregnant fooling around. Therefore, parents often need to create artificial consequences for both good and bad behavior.

Linking freedom to responsibility is an excellent approach. If your child is doing a great job of resisting peer pressure, extend her curfew a half hour. If she is dressing promiscuously, curtail some freedoms until her choices improve. If your son is losing his temper, suspend his driving privileges until he displays more self-control. In life, privilege is ultimately related to responsibility. Jail is the ultimate loss of privilege based on a lack of self-discipline. Teach your kids while they are young that the more they demonstrate self-control, the more freedom they will earn.

THE BEAUTY OF CONTENTMENT

I can say no to doughnuts, ice cream and even chocolate. But put a bag of chips in front of me and watch out. Sometimes when I find myself splurging on Doritos, I notice that I am stuffing a couple of chips at a time in my mouth and quickly devouring them. I can relate to the commercials that taunt, "Can't eat just one." Why can't I just savor a few and let it be?

Contentment and self-control are bedfellows. Feeling empty, unsatisfied and restless is a common precursor to almost all behavior that is uncontrolled. Our anger impatiently wants to create justice or bulldoze obstacles in our paths. Inappropriate sexuality is often a desperate, impulsive attempt to feel pleasure or connection with another person. Excesses of any kind seek to relieve anxiety and emptiness.

Teaching kids to be content with circumstances that are imperfect is a daunting task. Perhaps it begins with our own commitment to find and model contentment in plenty and with little. As parents we have many opportunities to teach kids that life is not fair and that their every desire is not meant to be fulfilled. Teaching this lesson is an uphill battle in a culture that constantly communicates the opposite. American enterprise is built on the strategy of creating wants and fulfilling desires. Nationwide contentment would render most advertisements futile.

Longings that are not impulsively gratified usually dissipate with time. That car you had to have a week ago is no longer a priority. The anger your daughter felt twenty minutes ago is now only mild irritation. Your son may have felt an incredible urge to cross the line with his girlfriend, but fifteen minutes later, he's perfectly happy watching a football game and talking to his friends. Contentment is a muscle that grows as we exercise it. Each time we say no to our yearnings for more, we affirm that we can be fulfilled without being indulged.

PRACTICING SELF-DISCIPLINE

Mark Twain is credited for giving this parenting advice: Put your children in a whiskey barrel and feed them through the hole. When they hit adolescence, plug up the hole. Sound tempting? Imagine all the trouble your kids could avoid if you locked them up between the ages of twelve and twenty!

Self-discipline comes with maturity. Young children have all their choices made for them. Adults make choices for themselves and others. A major task of childhood and adolescence is the transfer from parent discipline to self-discipline. Give a five-year-old unlimited access to junk food and video games, and he's sure to overindulge. Hopefully, a twenty-five-year-old would use some discretion.

When our kids reach young adulthood, they can feasibly have access to anything they want: drugs, alcohol, sex, pornography and guns. Will they have the discipline to make the right choices themselves, without our limits? Self-control is learned slowly as children are exposed to gradually increasing freedoms. Let your kids begin to make age-appropriate decisions that call for self-control.

Depending on the temperament and maturity of the individual child, here are some choices that most kids should be able to make:

Preschoolers—Get mad without hitting, ask for a cookie before taking it, wait to start eating until everyone is served.

Six to ten years old—Complete minor chores without supervision, work out arguments with some intervention, express anger without yelling, limit desserts and sweets, tell parent if inappropriate material is on television or in a movie.

Eleven to sixteen years old—Choose relatively balanced meals from a menu or buffet; recognize needs for sleep or food; keep track of school and household responsibilities; work out arguments without intervention; avoid peers who display problematic behaviors; avoid movies, video games and television with inappropriate ratings or material.

Seventeen to twenty years old—Plan for sleep and nutritional needs, balance responsibilities with leisure, demonstrate insight and appropriate control of anger, set limits for self related to sexual behavior, exercise judgment in choosing reading and viewing materials, recognize needs for accountability and seek peers with similar values.

Self-control is an ability that grows with practice. An eighteen-year-old who did not master the basics of self-control as a young child is ill-equipped to face the temptations of young adulthood. Teaching a rambunctious toddler the meaning of the word "no" is more important than some people think!

Proverbs that address self-control: anger—12:16; 13:16; 14:17, 29; 15:18; 17:27; 19:11, 19; 29:8, 11, 22; sexuality—5:3–23; 6:24–35; 7:4–27; 23:27–28; excess—10:1; 23:29–35

Self-Control

1. Think about each of your children. What areas of self-control are they currently struggling with?

_____

_____

2. How can you focus your influence to help your children develop the muscle of self-control?

_____

_____

EYE TO THE FUTURE

A simple man believes anything, but a prudent
man gives thought to his steps.

(Prov. 14:15)

The prudent see danger and take refuge, but
the simple keep going and suffer for it.

(Prov. 27:12)

Nothing seems more natural than to seek enjoyment and to seek it now. We hate pain and love pleasure. The ancient Greek philosophy of Epicureanism taught that wisdom comes from gratifying our bodily desires. After all, we are born with the compulsion to seek pleasure and avoid pain. You never have to teach a child to like sugar or to hate getting burned. One experience is enough. If this is true, then why do some people regularly spend hours running on a treadmill? Why would someone pass up a deliciously rich dessert or the opportunity to experience erotic sexual fantasies? We have choices. We can develop the ability to suspend our immediate desires in order to achieve a longer-range goal.

"Begin with the end in mind." One of Stephen Covey's seven habits of highly effective people resonates with Solomon's teaching in Proverbs. *Wisdom dictates that we learn to make decisions based on desired future outcomes rather than impulsive pleasure.*

Productivity, uncompromising integrity, restrained speech, positive peers, openness to feedback and self-control—none of them are important if there is no thought of tomorrow. A foundational principle of Proverbs (and of the whole Bible) is the concept of living today with tomorrow and eternity in mind.

The pleasure principle is a natural motivation for children. Try explaining to a four-year-old why he has to get painful vaccinations in order to prevent future illness. All the little guy knows is that he doesn't want to feel the pain of a shot today. Delayed gratification—forgoing something pleasurable now in order to avoid future pain—is one of the primary lessons we try to instill in our children.

Living with an eye to the future has two important applications: temporal and eternal. On the earthly level, kids must learn that what they do today has a direct impact on tomorrow. If they want a sterling report card in six weeks, they have to study now. If they want enough money to go camping in the fall, they have to save their summer earnings. If they want Mom and Dad to trust them in the future, they have to tell the truth now.

The second aspect of planning for the future is to embrace an eternal perspective. Being kind to an unpopular kid, giving money to the church, spending time in God's Word, resisting peer pressure, refusing to spread a piece of gossip . . . these may never be rewarded on earth, but God promises that He sees both the good and evil that are done in secret. Only by faith can we make decisions largely based on eternity.

Teaching our children to consider the future and eternal impact of their choices is a difficult but critical task.

Ideas for Encouraging an Eye Toward the Future

HELP PROJECT THE FUTURE

One reason kids have such a hard time delaying gratification is their limited ability to think about tomorrow. Young children are very concrete thinkers; all they know is the here-and-now. The capacity to think about tomorrow begins at around age three or four, but time is still a difficult concept to grasp. "How many sleeps until Christy comes to visit?" Andrew might ask. Although a child's ability to understand the future develops with time, even adolescents often fail to project consequences further than a couple of days. When you are fifteen, who cares about getting into college? That's way down the road. But the reality is that the grades a fifteen-year-old earns have a direct impact on the choices she will have when college approaches.

Parents have a role in helping remind their children of the future. Kids often need future consequences fleshed out for them. Obviously, this looks different depending on the stage of development. You may be teaching your son to be kind to others.

(Boys who fight with other kids won't have any friends to play with one day.) Maybe your seven-year-old is learning good eating habits. (You may want to eat pizza for breakfast, but it will give you a stomachache the rest of the day.) Your ten-year-old may be learning the benefits of productivity. (You may not feel like finishing your science fair project, but you'll be glad you did tomorrow when you get to go to the baseball game.) Your adolescent may be learning to control his anger. (It may feel great to tell off a teacher who made you mad, but the painful consequences will last a lot longer than the momentary satisfaction.)

Breaking consequences down into smaller segments can help a child link today's actions with their future impact. Say, for example, your seven-year-old hates to brush her teeth. You tell her over and over that if she doesn't brush, she may get a cavity. This is relatively meaningless to her as she has never had a cavity. The consequence is both unknown and at least several months away. But what if forgetting to brush results in no sweets for a week? Now the consequence is both immediate and meaningful.

"You told a lie! God's going to take a diamond off your crown!" If it's hard to get a child to think about next week, imagine the challenge of communicating an eternal perspective! Without consistent prompting, most kids never give eternity a second thought. Parents can help kids connect the dots with thoughtful questions or observations: "I know the kid you saw cheating on the test didn't get caught, but do you think God saw him?"

PRINCIPLE OF WORK BEFORE PLAY

A great way to teach delayed gratification is structuring pleasure as a reward for something productive. You probably do this without realizing it. "No dessert until you eat your dinner." "You can't go outside and play until your homework is done." "You can go to the basketball game when your room is clean."

This discipline, although pretty basic, is a building block for successful living. You don't get a paycheck unless you get to work at 7 A.M. every day. You won't have a good marriage unless you work on communication. Having a healthy body is the result of exercise and nutritious eating. Finishing difficult or less desirable tasks in order to gain something in the future is a habit that begins in childhood and is reinforced over time.

SEEK A BALANCED PERSPECTIVE OF TODAY AND THE FUTURE

Sometimes we can be so focused on teaching our children discipline and productivity, that we forget to allow them to enjoy and savor the gift of today. Proverbs teaches us that hard work is rewarded; don't forget to let your children enjoy the reward! If your kids are working hard, make sure they get a chance to play hard. If they are doing a good job, don't withhold praise.

Very few people find the appropriate balance between planning for the future and living in the present. You may know someone who is so good at delaying gratification that he delays it indefinitely. He eats tofu, runs five miles a day, gets up every morning at the crack of dawn and is productive until he can't possibly stay awake any longer. An appropriate perspective of the future also means realizing that life is fleeting. Youth and pleasure are with us for a season, and it's okay to enjoy the blessings God gives us.

> *What does a worker gain for his toil? I have seen the burden God has laid on men. He has made everything beautiful in its time. He has also set eternity in the hearts of men; yet they cannot fathom what God has done from beginning to end. I know that there is nothing better for men than to be happy and do good while they live. That everyone may eat and drink, and find satisfaction in all his toil—this is the gift of God.*
>
> (Eccl. 3:9–13)

Solomon's words speak of a balance—enjoying and working hard today, because tomorrow is not guaranteed. However, God has "set eternity" on our hearts. He has given us a glimpse of what *may* happen tomorrow and what *will* happen after this life. How difficult it is to make the most of today with an eye to both tomorrow and eternity!

As different as these seven pillars are, a common theme links them. You affect your children daily by what you emphasize, what you model, how you respond and what you directly teach. Proverbs has given us these important character traits as priorities for our parenting. Your actions and words as a mother are teaching your children something. As you build your blueprint, direct your influence toward what God's Word defines as wisdom and maturity.

Wisdom has built her house;
she has hewn out its seven pillars.

Proverbs 9:1

Proverbs that emphasize an eye to the future: 3:21–26; 4:25–27; 10:2, 24–25; 11:18, 23-28, 31; 12:3; 13:21; 14:8, 14–16; 15:24; 20:17, 22; 23:17; 24:19; 27:12, 23–27

Eye to the Future

1. On a scale from 1 to 5, how well do you think each of your children consider future consequences? _____

_____

2. How can you give your children a glimpse of living for eternity?

_____

3. On a scale of 1–5, how are each of your children developing in the seven areas of wisdom?

	Child's Name
Productivity	
Uncompromising Integrity	
Restrained Speech	
Positive Relationships	
Openness to Feedback	
Self-Control	
Eye to the Future	

4. How can you focus your influence to help your child develop?

_____

_____

6

Letting Go of
What You Never Had

Wisdom always works, except when it doesn't.

Laurie and Paul are the parents of two adult children. Both Laurie and Paul love God, love their children and truly have sought wisdom as they made parenting decisions. Yes, they are human and have made mistakes, but most who know them esteem them as wise, God-fearing people.

So, why, as they settle into retirement, are they riddled with grief and guilt about their children? Their firstborn, James, was their pride and joy. Always excelling and pleasing, he was easy to raise. He's now married and the father of a beautiful little girl. Yet, three months ago, James learned that he has a brain tumor. He was told to prepare to die within the year.

Their second child, Teresa, was strong-willed from the beginning. Throughout her childhood, Laurie and Paul did everything they knew to direct her will toward God. Although she had always chosen an unconventional road, she went off the deep end when she heard about her brother's illness. Her anger at God has consumed her. Now she is drinking heavily, out of work and living with a guy she met at a bar.

"What did we do wrong, Lord?" these faithful parents scream. "We tried to please you with our parenting. It wasn't supposed to turn out this way!"

The message of Proverbs is so empowering for parents. Proverbs promises that if we seek and apply wisdom, everything will turn out great. Unfortunately, Proverbs does not tell the entire story of wisdom. It speaks of principles, not promises.

Consider God's message to us in a few of the books that surround Proverbs. Job tells the story of a man who faithfully lived by wisdom but encountered the gravest of sorrows. Many of David's Psalms speak of his trials and depression in the midst of seeking God. The pessimism of Ecclesiastes follows the optimism of Proverbs and is perhaps the most depressing of all; Biblical scholars believe that Solomon wrote this book near the end of his life. Here's what he had to say:

> *"I devoted myself to study and to explore by wisdom all that is done under heaven. What a heavy burden God has laid on men! I have seen all the things that are done under the sun; all of them are meaningless, a chasing after the wind. What is twisted cannot be straightened; what is lacking cannot be*

counted. I thought to myself, 'Look, I have grown and increased in wisdom more than anyone who has ruled over Jerusalem before me; I have experienced much of wisdom and knowledge.' Then I applied myself to the understanding of wisdom, and also of madness and folly, but I learned that this, too, is chasing after the wind. For with much wisdom comes much sorrow; the more knowledge, the more grief."

(Eccl. 1:13–18)

The advanced lesson in wisdom is coming to terms with the limits of your wisdom. Yes, God calls you to be a wise mother. The wisdom that God gives you guides your children as they develop. *However, your wisdom does not ultimately determine the course of your children's lives.* There are elements of parenting you cannot control. What is wrong cannot be righted. What is missing cannot be recovered.

Acknowledging the limits of a mother's influence is scary, but it is essential to guilt-free motherhood. Many, many mothers feel responsible for elements of their children's lives that are far beyond their control. They may never be free from the grip of guilt until they clearly understand the limits of their responsibility for their children.

CONTROL VERSUS INFLUENCE

The other day I was watching my son play soccer. At his age, each kid has the chance to play all the different positions throughout the season. This particular day, Michael was the goalie. There was not much action at his end of the field, and he was dying to get into the game. He shouted directions at his teammates and paced at the very edge of the goal box. His frustration mounted as the play came near him, but not quite close enough. As if he could no longer contain his energy, Michael darted out of the goal box toward the action. The coach yelled from the sideline for him to go back to the goal, but Michael was too intent on being part of the play. Within a minute, the other team scored on the empty goal.

What a great example of the way I feel as a mom! God has given me a specific, unique role that is limited to the "goal box." Only I can "use my hands" in the game; no one else can do my job. I feel empowered when the play involves me. But often, the action occurs outside of my realm of influence. I get so frustrated when I cannot contribute! At times I give into the temptation to abandon my unique post and try to control the outcome. Like Michael, *I surrender my effectiveness when I don't recognize its limits.*

As mothers, we have tremendous influence with our children. But truth be told, most of us want more. We want control. We don't want to teach our children how to choose healthy foods; we want to make them eat exactly what we think they should. We don't want to influence whom they marry; we want to be the matchmaker. Teaching them values isn't enough; they may choose not to listen! We want to tell them how to dress, what to say, what to think and how to feel. If only we could write the perfect script for our children to follow, they would have perfect lives!

A fine line separates influence and control. God has given us one, not the other. We have great influence but no control. Ironically, grasping for control is the greatest threat

> We have great influence but no control. Ironically, grasping for control is the greatest threat to our influence.

to our influence. Guilt-free motherhood does not mean that you perfectly dictate the choices of your children. Instead, you strive to faithfully use your influence.

WHY WE WANT CONTROL

Most mothers readily agree to the logic that we cannot control our kids and sometimes have little power over their circumstances. However, acknowledging that fact logically and accepting it emotionally are two different things. Motherhood isn't exactly a logical endeavor.

One of the reasons that we cling to the illusion of control in our children's lives is that it gives us a false sense of power and security. Whenever I hear about a child growing in the wrong direction or suffering some kind of hardship, my mind immediately searches for the cause. When someone dies in a car accident, I ask, "Was he wearing his seatbelt?" A child experiments with drugs and I want to know, "Where did his parents fail him?"

Believing that a controllable cause for misfortune always exists assuages my fear that something bad could happen to my child. If rebellion and tragedy are random, then I feel completely helpless to prevent it. So, without exception I must project controllable variables on other parents whenever something bad happens.

Job's friends did exactly that as they watched their friend suffer. As you read their arguments, they sound so biblical. They applied great wisdom to his demise. A young Solomon may have agreed wholeheartedly with much of their counsel. They insisted, as we often do with others, that reaping tragedy is always the result of poor choices. They could not accept that Job's children were killed and he suffered hardship without deserving it. He must have been at least partially to blame. They pled with Job to repent and to turn to God for restoration. They encouraged him to see his own responsibility for his suffering. Surely, God would be blessing him if Job were as righteous as he claimed to be.

Their advice was limited to the sow/reap principles of wisdom, leaving no room for the many aspects of life that we cannot control. God did not appreciate the "wisdom" of Job's counselors. He said to one of them, "I am angry with you and your two friends, for you have not been right in what you said about me, as my servant Job has" (Job 42:7).

Do you ever wonder what parenting mistakes led to the misfortune of people you know? Drawing the wrong conclusions is so easy when we guess why some children turn out the way they do. We want to believe that parenting is an exact science and that we, therefore, can control the outcome of our children's lives.

There must be *something* you can do to guarantee that your baby avoids SIDS. You'll make *sure* your daughter never contracts cancer. No matter how hard you have to work, your children will *all* walk with the Lord. No son of *yours* will ever date the wrong girl.

The truth is that many variables besides parenting impact the life of a child. You can do everything right and still never be guaranteed happy, healthy, God-fearing children. By trying to control what you can't, you compromise the powerful role of motherhood. The wisdom of guilt-free motherhood is being fully devoted to your God-given influence while resting in the limits to it.

> The wisdom of guilt-free motherhood is being fully devoted to your God-given influence while resting in the limits to it.

CONGRATULATIONS!
YOU GAVE BIRTH TO A FREE WILL

The most obvious element of parenting that we cannot control is our children. Having young ones in the house, I am sometimes tempted to think that I have some control over my kids. They have to listen to me, right? I can custom-design their little lives. I cook their food, buy their clothes, determine bath time, drive them where I want them to go. . . . However, events remind me every day that my sense of control is only a facade. Yesterday, Andrew reminded me that I can set the bedtime, but I can't make him fall asleep. Christian proved that I can't make him stop crying in the middle of a traffic jam on the freeway. And Michael showed me that although I may have packed him chicken and an apple for lunch, he could choose to trade it for a bag of chips. The day is fast approaching when my futile attempts at control will be thrown back in my face.

Some are more forceful in how they do it, but all kids love to exercise their free will. Although they may want to please Mom, they don't want to be controlled by her. A child's ability and desire to make his own choices are facts of parenting. Nothing we can do changes this. So instead of compulsively or forcefully trying to *control* our children, let's shift our thinking toward how to most effectively *influence* their choices.

Your child's free will is not the enemy but a wonderful, albeit frightening, aspect of God's creation, part and parcel of the job of motherhood. Your influence is meant to be used for the purpose of molding and shaping that will. *Your goal is to teach your child to manage his free will, not to eliminate it.* Here are some ideas of how to help your child with the gift of free will that God has granted.

Give Room for Expression

All children, particularly adolescents, need to know that their parents respect their autonomy. Much of an adolescent's acting out is a statement about his or her desire to be treated as a grown-up. This very day, thousands of preteens and teens are telling their parents, "I'm not a little kid anymore. Stop treating me like a baby!"

What we realize but our children do not is how young ten, fifteen or twenty really is. The average teen knows just enough to get into really serious trouble. They may not look like little children, but they still need guidance, limits and protection. How does a parent encourage and respect a child's developing free will while still enforcing realistic, healthy parameters?

Allowing for and encouraging a child's ability to make decisions often takes away a child's need to make a statement about his autonomy. Starting with a toddler, there are many safe areas to allow a child to express his free will. He can choose a flavor of ice cream, which toy to take into the car and what color cup to have at lunch. As a child develops discretion and good judgment, the areas in which he is given choices should expand. Only give a child the choices that he is *capable* of making well. You want them to experience success at making decisions. This approach gives you the opportunity to regularly praise their judgment and decisions. If the amount of choices or the pressure is overwhelming, children are likely to fail. For example, taking a toddler into a store with thirty-one flavors and asking her to pick one is a recipe for a meltdown. Likewise, a thirteen-year-old is not ready to face the peer pressure of seventeen-year-old friends.

Sometimes we become so invested in trying to stay in control of our children that we forget the importance of their growing autonomy. Does it really matter if your son chooses to play chess over soccer? Or that your daughter doesn't want to try out for the school play? Although you may not like the choices your child makes, as long as they are not harmful, don't be critical. In fact, praise your child for his creativity and individuality. Your twelve-year-old daughter may go to school with a bright yellow shirt, purple pants, a blue belt and red patent-leather shoes. As long as she is not dressing immorally, let her express her autonomy through her wardrobe. You have many areas in which you should put your foot down, so don't sweat the choices that really don't matter (even if they drive you crazy!).

There also comes a time when children need to begin making moral decisions. "Mine!" and "No!" are often among the first utterances of tender youngsters. Whether we like it or not, children begin experimenting with moral choices even before they start walking! Will a ten-month-old touch the electrical outlet after Dad told him not to? Five-year-olds can lie or tell the truth. A second-grader can choose to be kind or rejecting to classmates. A ten-year-old can sass his mother. A teenager may choose to hang out with the wrong crowd, try drugs or drop out of school. Even if they are capable of making good choices, it doesn't mean that they always will. Scripture reminds us that we are all fallen and make rebellious and immoral choices. Yes, we can influence our children's choices, but we cannot ultimately decide for them.

The other day, I was walking through the mall with another mother, and we saw a group of adolescents dressed in baggy, black clothes with radical haircuts, smoking cigarettes—not an unfamiliar sight these days. As we strolled with our little ones past the motley crew, my friend commented, "I will never let my kids look like that!" I agreed wholeheartedly with her comment and shook my head in disgust at the unseen parents who contributed to this delinquency. Then the thought occurred to me, *How can I make sure that doesn't happen?* My mind fast-forwarded ten years to nightmarish arguments that might occur in our home.

"You're not going out of this house dressed like that, young man!"

"How are you going to stop me?"

Great question. How would I stop him? The terrifying truth is that ultimately I won't be able stop him from anything: running away, climbing out of his window dressed in whatever he wants, smoking at the mall, joining a cult, sleeping with his girlfriend, taking drugs. . . . As the saying goes, "Where there is a will there is a way." If he wants to badly enough, he will accomplish what he sets his mind on.

Discipline is so important to me as a mother because of this very reason: I want to respond wisely to my children's moral choices now. As they grow and develop, their moral choices become potentially more dangerous and overwhelming. Ultimately, I can do nothing to protect them from their free will; I can only help them learn to use it responsibly.

AVOID POWER STRUGGLES

When faced with the strength of a child's free will, a parent's natural inclination is to overpower their child. Taylor refuses to complete her family chores. Every Saturday morning when the family gets ready to clean the house, Taylor and Mom seem to get into a showdown. First, Taylor complains about how unfair her workload is. Then she mopes around the house, finding any distraction to keep her from her housework. Mom grows more and more frustrated as the day wears on. It is after 11:00, and the family needs to move on with their day. Everyone else has completed their chores, but Taylor has yet to begin.

As it has almost every Saturday, this battle has become personal. Taylor's defiance and rebellion have gotten under her mother's skin. In her mounting anger, Mom gives Taylor an ultimatum: "You are not leaving this house until your chores are done!" The battle has begun. Who will break first? Will Taylor finally get bored enough to attempt her chores? Will her mother really keep the rest of the family home all day until Taylor finishes? What happens if the chores still aren't done tomorrow? Will everyone stay home from church?

More often than we realize, we approach a child's free will by setting up power struggles. A power struggle is a battle of the wills; the more determined will win, and the less determined will lose. The struggle is by nature competitive rather than cooperative. Both parties become invested in not losing face. If the child "wins," the parent's authority is compromised. If the parent "wins," the child's self-confidence takes the hit. No ideal outcome exists in a power struggle, yet we find ourselves creating them all the time. We set out to prove that our own will is stronger than our child's.

The goal of a power struggle is to defeat a child's will to do something. A better alternative is giving choices with consequences. This strategy respects a child's free will, yet communicates the importance of responsibility and consequences. The difference between giving choices and creating a power struggle can be a fine line. However, the subtle difference communicates very different messages.

When we set up power struggles, we let our children know exactly what we are invested in them doing. For example, Taylor knows Mom will be irritated and angry until the chores are completed. Taylor is not really deciding whether or not to do her housework. She is really experimenting with the mother-daughter relationship. She wants to know how far she can push Mom. She may also feel very powerful to be able to get Mom so riled up. Taylor is getting a lot of attention and is dictating the entire family's afternoon by her actions.

Far healthier and more productive would be for Taylor's mom not to become invested in whether or not Taylor completes her chores. Instead, without becoming emotionally and personally involved, her mom can apply natural consequences to whatever choice Taylor makes. Her choices might look like this:

"Taylor, you are responsible for cleaning the bathroom, vacuuming your bedroom and cleaning all the windows. You have until noon to finish them. If you don't want to do them, then you can pay for someone else to do them. I will take thirty dollars out of your bank account to pay for getting the work done. It's up to you to decide." Or "If you choose not to contribute your part to the family workload, then you lose the privilege of having us do work that benefits you. Every Saturday your housework is not done by noon, your laundry will not be done that week and I will not drive you anywhere other than school and church."

Do you see the subtle difference between a power struggle and providing choices? This strategy also mirrors God's relationship with us. He could out-muscle and control us completely. Instead, He respects our free will by giving choices with clear consequences.

We can influence choices by the consequences we assign to them. We can make one choice much more appealing than the others. By giving a child choices and consequences, we are teaching them good judgment in the use of their free will. Rather than becoming helpless victims of circumstances, they become empowered to take responsibility for their behavior.

ALLOW THEM TO EXPERIENCE CONSEQUENCES

Many parents see the wisdom in giving choices but fall short of effective parenting because they interfere with the consequences of choices. This trap is very easy to fall into. Ten-year-old Johnny forgets his book report at home. He calls from the school pleading for Mom to bring it in for him. The consequence of his forgetfulness will be a lowered grade. What should Mom do? Lovingly come to his rescue, or allow him to feel the pain of his irresponsibility?

Most of us shortcut our children's consequences far more

often than we realize. Watching our children suffer hardship is very difficult, because we naturally want to come to their defense. We even release them from the consequences that we have given them. A child who was grounded for a week suddenly earns "parole" after two days of good behavior.

Life is not so sympathetic with consequences. If a grown child chooses to come to work late every day, his boss is unlikely to show mercy. If he forgets to make his mortgage payments, the bank does not come to his aid.

Many parents feel guilty because they assume responsibility for their children's choices. Mothers are only responsible to be faithful with their *own* choices for their children. When a mom takes responsibility for her children's poor decisions, she interferes with the child's sense of accountability.

A mother talks to her fourteen-year-old daughter who was caught shoplifting. "I know I've been busy and haven't been around for you enough lately. Maybe this is your way of getting my attention."

Although the mother's negligence may have been a contributing factor to her daughter's behavior, the girl is solely responsible for her own conduct. Excusing her by taking the guilt subtly teaches the young girl to pass the blame of her own responsibility onto others.

One of the most important lessons we can teach our children is that there are *always* consequences for the choices they make. They literally can do whatever they want, but they cannot escape the ramifications of their actions.

The whole concept of punishing children is creating artificial consequences that mirror natural consequences. There is, for example, no immediate consequence for telling a lie. A child can usually get away with little fibs for years without feeling the effects of broken trust. However, the wise parent creates an immediate consequence so the child begins to associate the behavior with a negative reaction.

Experts believe the best consequences, or punishments, are those that are most closely related to the behavior. Sometimes, the behavior lends itself to consequences as long as the parent doesn't intervene. Refusing to eat what Mom served for lunch should result in hunger. Irresponsibility leads to a loss of freedom. Fighting with others calls for isolation.

We do our children no great favors when we shortcut the consequences of their actions. The stakes only become higher as they age. We must let them learn the painful lessons of life while they are young.

Along with negative consequences for poor choices, providing positive consequences for good choices is also important. We can easily become so engrossed in responding to bad behavior that we forget to reward and praise our children for the good choices they make. A child may make fifty good decisions in a day and two bad decisions. Usually the bad choices are the ones that come to Mom's attention. She never gets a note from school telling her that her son used self-control when another child cut in front of him. She doesn't even notice when siblings play together cooperatively for hours without fighting.

Experts suggest that parents aim to give their children ten praises for every criticism. In reality, a mother's words are usually dominated by scolding and correction. (I know mine tend to be!) It takes effort to catch your children being good. But if we look, I would guess that the good choices far outweigh the bad.

LET GO

Letting go. Boy, I'm not looking forward to this one. Accepting that my children's lives are not mine is so difficult. Each one of them may ultimately make choices that contradict everything I believe. They may choose to put themselves in harm's way. They may live lives filled with painful consequences, and I may feel completely helpless to do anything about it.

As I observe mothers of adult children, I see many who are not willing to accept this fact. As they feel their influence dwindling, they become desperate. They may manipulate with money, emotions, withholding love—trying frantically to cling to some control over their children's lives. I see others racked by regret, disappointment and guilt—unwilling to let go of their role in their children's destiny. I can't say I blame them. I can't say that I won't be tempted to do the same. Letting go is not easy!

You may be right in the middle of letting your child go. No words can adequately describe how difficult this action may be for you. No simple formula is available to make it less personal, painful or terrifying. Slamming right up to the limits of your influence is perhaps the greatest challenge for a mother. After caring so greatly, loving so deeply and investing so much, how can you possibly stop and let your child walk deeper into life without you? Although your mind knows that letting go is the right thing to do, your heart is screaming for you to grab control of the uncontrollable.

Carol Wichowski's empty-nest syndrome
takes a turn for the worse.

Reprinted by permission of John McPherson, as appeared in Chicken Soup for the Soul Cartoons for Moms.

By refusing to let go, you make your child's life a drama about mother and child. The decisions he makes will be motivated by either pleasing Mom or trying to break away from her, which interferes with maturity and overshadows a child's relationship with God. Rather than evaluating decisions in light of his parent's opinion, a young adult needs to seek God's direction.

We can only truly release our children when we remember that parenting is a ministry and a calling. Parenting is a job granted by the Almighty, not an identity. We are not primarily mothers. We are first and foremost the daughters of God. We parent to please Him and to experience His pleasure. As our children grow (and someday outgrow us), we must trust God to shepherd us into other avenues of ministry. Although we love our children deeply, they cannot become our obsession or the source of our significance.

Another difficult aspect of letting go is releasing the results of parenthood. Stan and Dana have four children, ranging from age twenty-seven to age eighteen. Only in the past few years have Stan and Dana devoted their lives to Christ. Throughout most of their years of marriage and parenting, they struggled through trying to do the best for their children based on their own wisdom. Looking back, they realize some mistakes they made and wish they could parent all over again from a godly perspective. They wonder how their failures are now affecting their children, two of whom want nothing to do with God. Their lifestyles and choices grieve Stan and Dana. *God, is it too late?* they wonder. *Did we fail so miserably that our children will never seek You?*

Oh, how the heart of a prodigal's mother must break! Proverbs 10:1 says, "A wise son brings joy to a father; but a foolish child brings grief to a mother." A primary source of guilt in motherhood is grieving over the negative results in our children's lives. Sure, God calls us to parent wisely. But we also know that none of us can perfectly accomplish that task. If our children don't turn out the way we desire, how do we cope with the guilt and blame of our mistakes?

We influence our children but do not control them. We cannot be responsible for their choices. At some point we must let go of our failures and stop blaming ourselves for every flaw we see in our children. God knows that we are not perfect. He chose to give us our children, as imperfect as we may be. He knows our mental, physical and emotional limitations. He also holds our children accountable for their *own* moral and spiritual choices. Many people who have come from terrible home situations are fully honoring God through their lives. Others raised in close to ideal circumstances deny their need for God.

It is never too late for you to pray for your children, nor to share the hope of Christ with them! Seek wisdom, cry out for His help and give it your best today. You do not have to be shackled by the mistakes you may have made. Let go of the need to be perfect and the responsibility of raising perfect children. God only wants you to be faithfully devoted to Him today, wherever you may be, and to release the results to Him. Let Him carry your grief.

Let us then approach the throne of grace with confidence,
so that we may receive mercy and find grace to help us in
our time of need.

(Heb. 4:16)

Only God Is God

You may be able to choose where your children go to school, influence their choice of friends and help them decide on a career. But do you realize that you have no influence over whether or not they take another breath? As a mom, you affect your kids in important ways. However, you can never determine God's ultimate plan for them.

Motherhood often goes smoothly. We apply the principles of wisdom and see our children mature. We feel empowered, capable and grateful. Then the unexpected happens. We come face-to-face with the limits of our wisdom and influence. Realizing that our wisdom has no control over the most critical aspects of our children's lives can be frightening.

The ultimate limit of our influence is that we cannot control God.

Whatever exists has already been named, and what man is
has been known; no man can contend with one who is
stronger than he.

(Eccl. 6:10)

Do you know that God has numbered the days of your children? He determined from their conception everything about their looks, their personality and their part in His plan. David wrote:

> My frame was not hidden from you when I was made in the secret place. When I was woven together in the depths of the earth, your eyes saw my unformed body. All the days ordained for me were written in your book before one of them came to be.
>
> (Ps. 139:15–16)

Do you find God's sovereignty comforting or scary? Do you trust God's plan for the little children you have grown to love so dearly?

Trusting God with Our Children

I think the ultimate irony of motherhood is this: God trusts us with His children, yet we don't trust Him with ours.

Feeling guilty as a mother is a product of knowing how fallen and limited we are. Try as we may, we are never perfect. Yet God has chosen to entrust these precious lives into our care. We look at God's awesome power and wisdom. In spite of His love and faithfulness we often doubt whether we can trust Him with the very children that He gave us!

I am certain that you can think of godly parents you know whose children have suffered hardship and perhaps even death. While a fifteen-year-old drug addict has a healthy child, a loving

Christian couple gives birth to a severely handicapped child. You wonder, *Why didn't God protect those who honor Him?*

Every mother must ultimately wrestle with trusting her children to God. It's easy to lean on Him when we believe that He always protects them from pain and harm. But what if He doesn't? How can we trust Him when there is no promise of security and happiness for our children?

The events of September 11, 2001, brought this home for all of us. On the days following the tragedy, we didn't care about the little battles we fight every day. We just wanted to hold and protect our kids. In our helplessness, we had to turn to God, acknowledging that only He determines our future. We were reminded of Scripture like Psalm 23, "Even though I walk through the valley of the shadow of death, I will fear no evil, for you are with me." But how can we not fear death and pain for our children? How can we confidently stride into tomorrow not knowing what tragedy might await our kids?

A Bigger Picture

The pinnacle of wisdom is recognizing how limited our understanding truly is. We know what seems "good" for our children. What God allows to happen sometimes seems far from "good."

> *He has made everything beautiful in its time. He has also put eternity into man's mind, yet so that he cannot find out what God has done from the beginning to the end.*
> (Eccl. 3:11)

God's ways are so far beyond our understanding. He has a picture that is so much greater than the present. He has given us just a glimpse of eternity to remind us of how much greater His wisdom is than ours. Do we really believe that we can parent better than God? From our limited perspective, the answer may be yes.

If God would grant me ultimate control over my children, I know I would spare them from pain and hardship. I could script a wonderful life for them. But in doing so, my will, even though well intentioned, would interfere with God's plan for my children's lives. He has created them for His purpose, which is so far beyond my understanding. Imagine if Mary had the power to script her son's life. Surely, being a loving and protective mother, she would have spared Jesus from the pain and humiliation of the cross. But in doing so, she would have thwarted the very purpose of His life.

Your fifteen-year-old cannot imagine why it wouldn't be good for her to go out with the eighteen-year-old star of the football team. Your decision to say no seems cruel and unjust. But you have a much more complete understanding of her safety and future. Try as you may to explain your concerns, she probably won't understand until she sees through a parent's eyes. Although she may view you as uncaring, your decision was made out of love.

The same is true of God. His ways may seem cruel and untrustworthy. But we cannot understand the bigger picture. What do you want to change about your children or their lives? What circumstances has God allowed that seem far from good? What keeps you from trusting Him completely with the future of your children? How do you try to "help" God forge a better plan?

Although we gave birth to our children, we are not the author of their lives. When we try to control, we only mess things up. Rebekah is a great example of this. She had twins, Jacob and Esau. When she was pregnant with the boys, she felt them fighting inside of her. She asked God why and He answered, "Two nations are in your womb, and two peoples from within you will be separated; one people will be stronger than the other, and the older will serve the younger" (Gen. 25:23). Although God had told Rebekah that Esau would serve Jacob, we see her fear that this would not happen. She deceived her husband, Isaac, to make sure that Jacob received his blessing! As we are often tempted to do, Rebekah thought God needed her help to fulfill His promise. She abandoned principles of godly wisdom to control the outcome.

We have the luxury of reading biblical stories from beginning to end. We read about Sarah and her doubts about having Abraham's promised son. We shake our heads at her effort to manipulate the situation by giving her handmaid to Abraham. But what was it like for her to watch the years pass without God's answer?

Do you truly believe that God has a plan for your kids? Do you believe that He is greater than your doubts or fears?

Most of this book has addressed the tremendous influence you have as a mom. However, your influence is wasted if you use

> Your influence is wasted if you use it trying to interfere with God's purpose and work in your children's lives.

it trying to interfere with God's purpose and work in your children's lives. They were not born for the purpose of making you happy or fulfilled. They were born only for His purpose. The days of happiness, joy, warm hugs and smiles are a gift to be savored, but are not the ultimate reason we have children.

Guilt-free motherhood is not about fervently clinging to our children, but faithfully releasing them. Consider the lives of each of these children:

- ♡ Daniel: The Babylonians defeated his country when he was a teenager. They tore him away from his family and brought him to Babylon. He probably never saw his parents again.
- ♡ Joseph: His mother died when Joseph was a small boy. At seventeen, he was thrown into a pit by his jealous brothers. Then he was sold as a slave, taken to Egypt and spent many years in prison.
- ♡ David: As a young boy he defeated Goliath with a slingshot. Saul made him live in the palace and did not allow him to return home. Then he spent much of his young adulthood alone, hiding in the wilderness to escape Saul.
- ♡ Esther: Her parents both died when she was a young child. She was raised by her uncle Mordechai and was taken into

the Persian king's palace as a young teenager. Eventually she became queen.

♡ Samuel: His mother, Hannah, dedicated him to the Lord. She brought him to the temple to be raised by the priest Eli when he was about three years old.

♡ Moses: Pharaoh passed a law that all Hebrew infants would be killed when he was born. His mother placed him in a basket in the Nile River (can you imagine doing that with your baby?). Through God's grace, she was his wet nurse until Moses was weaned. Then he lived in the palace with Pharaoh's daughter as his mother.

What did all of these heroes have in common? Way before we would think it was time, they were torn from their homes. In each case, their parents were faithful with the few days they had with their children. The Bible doesn't record the grief and fear that each of these mothers must have felt. We only see that God worked dramatically in the lives of their children. They each belonged to God, and each was released into His sovereign care "for such a time as this!"

Godly wisdom ultimately prompts us to consider a paradigm shift. Parenting isn't about us. It's not about our kids. The goal is not long life and happiness. We understand these things as good, but they are not God's best! Becoming lost in the good things of motherhood can blind us to God's ultimate purpose in parenting.

What it all boils down to is this: We live to love God and bring glory to His name whatever the circumstances. Yes, we seek and apply the wisdom of Proverbs to our interactions. We strive to build strong, loving relationships with our children. We work toward instilling character in their lives. But we realize that the final goal is to achieve God's purpose in their lives and ours. We only have a glimpse of that purpose and trust Him for direction. His plan may be very different from what we want or hope, but we trust that what may be scary and painful is within His control.

He knows your limits as a mother. He knows your child's medical conditions. He knows every circumstance. He is not surprised. Your child is not too tall, too shy, too sick or too clumsy to accomplish God's plan.

> *And we know that in all things God works for the good of those who love him, who have been called according to his purpose.*
>
> (Rom. 8:28)

What more could I want for my children than for each of them to have a passion and hunger for God's work in their lives? But this desire means that I must wean them from Mom-dependence to God-dependence. My love, my care, my wisdom and my limitations must all point them to God's love, care, wisdom and perfection! In my flesh, I want to hold their hands so tightly that they can never wiggle free, but I must loosen my grip if I am ever to place their hands in God's.

Much of the anxiety and guilt of motherhood arises because of our stubbornness at accepting the limits of our control. What goals do you have for parenting? Most of us appraise our motherhood based on goals that overreach our areas of influence. "I want my children to be. . . ." You fill in the blank. Successful, confident,

> Much of the anxiety and guilt of motherhood arises because of our stubbornness at accepting the limits of our control.

godly, happy. These goals are all ones over which we have no control. We often evaluate our job performance based on something outside of our realm of influence. No wonder mothers feel guilt-ridden and fearful!

As a mother, you can use your influence in a manner that *encourages* certain outcomes, *but you cannot create any outcome!* Any goal of motherhood that is not directly related to your attitudes and behavior is an inappropriate goal and causes you to strive toward something you cannot control. Dreaming, hoping and praying for your child's future or development is wonderful, but your focus in this drama must be on your faithfulness in *your* role, not anyone else's! Striving toward what you cannot control distracts you from the true goal of motherhood: faithfully and wisely devoting your influence in parenting as an act of service to the Lord.

*A man's steps are directed
by the Lord. How then can anyone
understand his own way?*

Proverb 20:24

For Personal Reflection

1. In what areas of parenting do you feel frustrated about not having control? _____

   _____

2. Think about your experience growing up. How did your mother do with "letting you go"? Giving you choices? Providing consequences for your choices? _____

   _____

3. What are some appropriate areas in each of your children's lives that you can give them room to make choices and express their autonomy? _____

   _____

4. In what areas of your children's lives do you fear trusting God?

   _____

Part III

What Do I Do
with My Guilt?

7

Avoiding the Vomit

So, you have a plan for guilt-free motherhood. You know the importance of parenting through godly wisdom. You want to seek God's direction, trusting that He will grant it. You also understand and accept the limits of your influence and wisdom. Are you now certain to parent without the shadow of guilt?

Unfortunately, the answer may be no. Most of us have a vast storehouse of information on the right thing to do in almost any situation, yet we stumble throughout the parenting process, in spite of access to the treasure of wisdom. Why? How few people find wisdom and even fewer live by her! Proverbs 14:1 says, "The wise woman builds her house, but with her own hands the foolish one tears hers down." Why is it so difficult to be a wise woman? Why do so many of us end up tearing down the most precious people in our lives?

Throughout Proverbs, Solomon refers to two different kinds of people who do not have wisdom: fools and the simple-minded. Unlike fools, the simpleminded (or naive) person doesn't know any better. A good example may be a nineteen-year-old mother of twins. Married, then pregnant, right out of high school, this poor woman is naturally overwhelmed. What does she know about raising children or managing a household? If she doesn't have significant help from her mother or another mentor, she is likely to make some critical mistakes out of ignorance.

Naiveté is not limited to the young. Plenty of middle-aged or elderly people by choice or because of legitimate limitations do not have the information they need to be wise. They have difficulty discerning good advice from bad and often place their children at the mercy of the untrustworthy.

The foolish, on the other hand, have access to wisdom but stubbornly refuse to listen to her. For one reason or another, their hearts are hardened toward wisdom. They may be kind and loving, but they want to do things their own way. Such stubbornness seems to be part of our sin nature. If we were honest, we would probably all admit pockets of our lives that speak of foolishness—habits we refuse to give up, self-disciplines we lack, advice that we resent.

"As a dog returns to his vomit, so a fool returns to [her] folly" (Prov. 26:11). If you have ever had a dog, you know what

Solomon is referring to. Dogs have an instinct to clean up their own vomit. What a disgusting word picture! But it drives home the point of our own bizarre actions. Why are we drawn to repeat foolish, destructive behavior? Why do we give in to our children's demands when we know it is wrong? Why do we yell and verbally berate them when we are angry? Why do we refuse to enforce consistent boundaries? Why do we fight with our husbands in front of the kids? Without wisdom, we make the same mistakes over and over again, drowning in the guilt of "I should have known better!"

A forty-six-year-old man suffers a major heart attack. The near-death experience naturally scares him. *From now on,* he promises himself, *I'm going to take my health seriously.* The doctor recommends daily exercise, a low-fat and low-sodium diet, and significant lifestyle changes to reduce stress. "If you don't make these changes," the doctor warns, "the next heart attack will kill you." The man is dedicated to the new routine for about a month. As the memory of lying on a hospital gurney begins to fade, so does his commitment to change. Slowly, he returns to his old habits. The danger has not dissipated, but the warning has been replaced by life's allure.

What a foolish man, you think. But don't we do the same thing? When our children's behavior creates a salient problem, we are at wisdom's door asking for help. We want the pain and the danger to go away. As soon as the threat has faded into the horizon, wisdom becomes an annoying mother-in-law, bugging us with unwanted advice.

"I know I should _____ ,
but _____ . . ."
You fill in the blanks. We've all said it, or at least thought it.
Suddenly the fool Solomon so often refers to in Proverbs doesn't
seem so abstract. Wisdom is readily available to us, but so often
we don't want her. We ignore her and sometimes even despise
her. Why?

THE TRAP OF PRIDE

Perhaps the most profound example of foolishness is
Solomon himself. How sad to read about the ending of
Solomon's life. He was blessed with great wisdom, yet rejected
the very principles he taught.

Solomon experienced great success as a result of his wisdom.
He was the richest, most powerful man in the world. The Bible
tells us that kings came from everywhere to marvel at his wisdom and accomplishments. Solomon's behavior indicates that
his giftedness and his wisdom became his confidence. He began
to trust in himself rather than in God. His own words fore-
shadowed his ultimate heartbreaking conclusion, "Pride comes
before destruction, and a haughty spirit before a fall" (Prov.
16:18).

The Lord knew Solomon's heart and warned him against
marrying foreign wives. "'You must not intermarry with them,
because they will surely turn your hearts after their gods.'
Nevertheless, Solomon held fast to them in love. . . . As

Solomon grew old, his wives turned his heart after other gods, and his heart was not fully devoted to the LORD his God" (1 Kgs. 11:2–4). After spending most of his lifetime building a majestic temple for the Lord, in his old age Solomon built altars to false gods. His heart was rebellious before God, and he failed to turn from his foolishness. Why? What went wrong? How did this man of tremendous wisdom become so foolish?

Wisdom begets success. Success begets pride. Pride begets foolishness. The greatest block to listening to wisdom is pride. We simply think we know better. We trust our own gut, our own wisdom, our own experience. We don't need help. Like Solomon, we can start out seeking wisdom and gradually slide into self-reliance as we experience success. How easily we can forget to glorify God for successes rather than concluding, "I must be a good mother." Pride is the archenemy of wisdom. As soon as we trust ourselves, we are blind and deaf to wisdom's cry to sit at the feet of the Master. "Do you see a man wise in his own eyes? There is more hope for a fool than for him" (Prov. 26:12).

Staying focused on wisdom is only possible when we are invested in seeking God through the *process* of parenting rather than evaluating our success in the *result* of parenting. When our passion is to achieve great results, we fluctuate between pride and guilt daily as our children switch between good and bad behavior. We may feel very proud of raising one child and like a complete failure while raising another. Both extremes are destructive to God's purposes in our lives and our children's lives.

Why do we only tend to seek wisdom when there is a specific problem with our children? Because when motherhood is running smoothly, we conclude that we don't really need to seek God's help. We're doing fine on our own. We trust in our own strength and wisdom, and our hearts are led astray to seek guidance from ungodly sources. As soon as we trust our own ability to discern right from wrong, we become vulnerable to all kinds of evil. We begin to pay homage to materialism, intelligence, popularity and pleasure.

Wisdom is like manna. God seems to give us just what we need for today. Our responsibility is to gather it and digest it. But storing extra wisdom today does not save us from becoming foolish tomorrow. Each day of motherhood is a new opportunity to seek God or to reject His wisdom.

Change Is Too Hard

Another reason that many fail to implement wisdom is that it requires hard work. Megan and Brian have three children, ages seven, five, and three. They love their kids as much as any parents can. In fact, their lives seem to revolve around their children. The food they eat, vacations they take, where they go to church—practically all decisions are made to keep their kids happy.

For example, Amanda, the oldest, hates going to the grocery store. Any time she has to accompany Mom or Dad grocery shopping, she whines and complains. Megan and Brian find themselves bending over backward to accommodate her. They try to arrange their schedules so that Amanda never has to go to the store. If that doesn't work, they appease her. "I'm sorry, Amanda. I tried to get to the grocery store when you were at school but I ran out of time. Let me buy you some special treats for coming to the store with me."

The grocery store is just one example. All three kids know how to get their way. Mom and Dad are running themselves ragged to make sure the kids are happy. Sometimes they even serve three different things for dinner because Amanda likes hot dogs, Chad likes PB and J, and Kelly likes mac and cheese.

Friends and family tactfully bring to the couple's attention that perhaps they are too focused on serving their children. They have read books that teach loving discipline, yet they continue to foster whining, pouting and selfishness.

Catering to them is how Brian and Megan know how to love their children. They genuinely believe they are being good parents by knocking themselves out for their kids. It is not natural for them to say no or to let their children cry from not getting their way. Stricter parents seem harsh and uncaring to them.

Surely, Brian and Megan want to be good parents. They don't want to harm their kids, so why are they impervious to the mistakes they are making? Calling them foolish seems harsh, but they ignore the wisdom that could make them better parents and build character in their children.

Brian and Megan have their parenting system down, and it seems to "work" for them. Changing the way they interact with the kids and how they make decisions would be a challenging adjustment. They are too busy and frazzled to consider making such a drastic change. They can easily rationalize the mistakes they make by looking at the many ways in which they are excellent and loving parents.

Although our blind spots may be different, we can probably all relate to areas in which we as mothers stubbornly refuse to listen to wisdom. Maybe you favor one child over another, are quick to lose your temper, don't want to let go of control, foster power struggles or overuse electronic baby-sitters. Based on your own unique personality, experiences and situation, following godly wisdom is very challenging in some aspects of parenting. If you are controlling, letting go presents an awesome challenge. If you are lax and undisciplined, being consistent and organized can feel like swimming upstream. The truth is that genuine change is *difficult!* As a result, we continue to make the same mistakes over and over again, hoping that our strengths can compensate for our natural weaknesses.

> *Though you grind a fool in a mortar, grinding him like grain with a pestle, you will not remove his folly from him.*
> (Prov. 27:22)

THERE IS NO "I" IN MOTHERHOOD

Why is change so difficult? We never parent randomly but always out of our own longings and passions. Truly embracing wisdom means that we let go of profound, often unconscious needs that we cling to in motherhood.

Motherhood naturally meets some needs of companionship and significance for any mother. What mom doesn't hope that her child will make her proud or will always love to spend time with her and value her? Far too often, these natural desires take over parenting, overriding our commitment to wisdom.

I doubt if any mother has never wrestled with her own selfish needs while parenting. Mothers have so much power with their children that they naturally set the tone for the mother-child relationship. Without the constant power of God in our lives, we subconsciously form the parenting relationship based on what we need or want. Most of the time, we don't even realize how much we depend on our children to meet our emotional needs and how stubbornly we cling to foolish patterns.

We can only be guilt-free when we embrace the fact that motherhood is never about us. Children are not vehicles through which we meet our needs. Instead, motherhood is an amazing opportunity to both experience and express the unconditional love of Christ.

As you read the following caricatures, you will probably recognize these traits in mothers that you know. Most importantly, be aware of your own tendency to forge a parenting style around your emotional needs.

Successful Sydney

If Sydney sends one message over and over again to her children, it is, "Make me proud." She never says these exact words, but her children understand the meaning nonetheless. Appearances have always been important to Sydney. Her children, after all, are a reflection of her. Others, in her mind, perceive her as successful only when her children shine. Sydney's daughter wonderfully obliges. She is diligent and respectful, and she naturally excelled in school and later in business. Unfortunately, Sydney's son is not so cooperative. As hard as she tries, Sydney can never convince her son to take anything seriously. Always feeling compared to his sister, he refuses to try to compete for Mom's stamp of approval. Instead, he pursued his own passions: music and kayaking. As an adult, he became a music teacher and band director for a local high school. During the summers, he takes off to the Rockies to hike and kayak. While Sydney frequently boasts about her daughter's accomplishments, seldom does she mention her son's "disappointing" choices. In her estimation, one child is a success while the other has failed to make her proud.

Let's face it; your children are a reflection of you. Their success makes you look and feel successful. When they fail, you see yourself as a failure. Most mothers daydream about what their children will someday be like. Although wanting your children to be your "pride and joy" is natural, it is not the motivation God calls us to as mothers. When raising "successful" children becomes our goal, we can stubbornly refuse to yield to God's plan. We also run the risk of projecting our own dreams onto our children without letting them discover their own.

What clothes they wear, what jobs they get, what grades they earn, how they perform athletically, whom they marry, how many children they have—these are all ways a mom can subtly define the "success" of her child and consequently her own adequacy.

When soccer moms go too far.

Reprinted by permission of John McPherson, as appeared in Chicken Soup for the Soul Cartoons for Moms.

Inappropriately defining success isn't always about materialism. Some parents favor children who enter full-time ministry, who follow in the family business or who fulfill a dream that the parent was unable to attain. In each case, these parents use their approval as a carrot. They communicate conditional love based on fulfilling goals that have nothing to do with following God's leading. Such a mom can become so entrenched in seeing her kids succeed that she is blind to her own foolishness.

Victoria the Victim

Victoria's motto (which is no secret!) is "Poor me! I have it so hard!" While Sydney likes to brag about how good her children are, Victoria constantly complains about how rotten hers are. "You won't believe what Shawn did yesterday! He got suspended from school again for graffiti. And when I tried to punish him, he threw his clock radio out the window and threatened to run away. He's just like his father. All I've ever done is love him, and look at what grief he is giving me! What did I do to deserve this?!"

Victoria likely started motherhood with visions of being a great mother. But as time passed and she experienced more failure, Victoria began to give up. For a woman who feels completely overwhelmed and incapable, the victim role is a seductive way of having her needs met. Instead of being defensive about parenting mistakes, Victoria moans about how dreadful her home is. In this way, she averts responsibility and gains sympathy from others.

"Poor, Victoria," her friends whisper. "She must be so miserable. You couldn't pay me enough to switch places with her!"

Rather than dealing with her own feelings of inadequacy, Victoria projects the blame to her children, which naturally sends an incredibly damaging message to her children: "You're no good." She may try to explain all of her children's problems by diagnoses like attention deficit disorder or oppositional defiant disorder to further emphasize that she has no responsibility for her children's poor behavior.

Counseling Victoria is no fun. Victims are never interested in wisdom; they only want sympathy. To admit that they are capable of change means accepting responsibility for the past and for the present. Therefore, Victoria works overtime to convince anyone peddling wisdom that "I have tried it all before," but it never worked for her because she has it so much harder than anyone else.

Victoria probably has some very legitimate limitations that impact her parenting. Maybe she began life as a victim of abuse, a dysfunctional home, an unwanted pregnancy. Perhaps she struggles with depression, bipolar disorder, chronic pain or another physiological disorder. But instead of leaning on God's strength and sovereignty, Victoria gives in to defeat. She doesn't believe that God's grace and strength are truly sufficient. "Surely, wisdom is not accessible to me," she reasons.

Scripture tells us that we are accountable for that which we are given, whether it be a lot or a little (Luke 12:48). Perhaps you have very little to give as a mother. Remember the widow who only had a mite (or a penny) but gave it to God. Jesus said, "I tell you the truth, this poor widow has put more into the treasury than all the others. They gave out of their wealth; but she, out of her poverty, put in everything—all she had to live on" (Mark 12:43–44). God knows how much you have to offer your children. It's okay if you feel empty. But give it all to Him and watch Him bless it. In the words of Winston Churchill, "Never, never, never, never give up."

Mae the Martyr

Like Victoria, Mae wants other people to recognize how difficult her life is—not because she is a victim, but because she is a saint. Mae is willing to sacrifice anything at any time for her children. She works so hard to be a great mom. She drives them everywhere, cleans up after them, spends hours cooking gourmet meals and goes to every sporting event. She believes that if she works hard and sacrifices enough, then the ending has to be good. What she wants most is to be appreciated for her sacrifices. Therefore, she's afraid to ever say no. Subconsciously, Mae reasons, *The more I sacrifice, the more they will love me.* When her children begin to slip away emotionally or disappoint her, she reminds them of the love and appreciation they owe her.

Most people would never see Mae as selfish. On the contrary, she appears to be the most giving and selfless person around. She is always willing to lay down her needs and desires for her loved ones. But Mae sacrifices not out of love, but out of need. Each sacrificial act is a deposit in the bank of her children—an emotional string tied from her to them. She will someday make withdrawals to get what she wants and needs from her children. It may be a pout, a deep sigh or strategically placed statement, "Don't worry about me. I'm fine," that reminds her kids that "you owe Mama!"

Often not until her children reach adolescence or adulthood does someone like Mae realize her own calculating motives for serving. While her children are young, Mae receives wonderful rewards for her sacrifices. Her children praise her and shower her with affection. But when the payback turns into backtalk and rejection, Mae becomes angry. Her ears are deaf to wisdom's call.

Motherhood certainly is the job of a servant. But remember, true servants give of themselves out of devotion, never to gain leverage. Guilt-free motherhood means serving the Lord with your whole heart through parenting without regard to what you get back. The Lord loves and blesses the cheerful giver, not the manipulative one.

Controlling Carol

Raising a child can be a chaotic task. Women who love structure may go berserk with a two-year-old covered in chocolate running around the house, a seven-year-old who refuses to change his underwear and a teenager who wants to pierce every imaginable body part. A common response to the unpredictable nature of motherhood is to cling to control in the midst of chaos.

Neatness, cleanliness, diet, fitness, schedules and manners are all areas in which Carol can feel some semblance of power. Controlling the tangibles can become a tempting compensation for all the intangibles that create anxiety. Carol can't make her kid love God, but she can make him attend church four times a week.

The things that Carol focuses on are good things! Schedules, healthy food, being on time, completing chores and obeying rules are foundational to effective parenting. However, Carol takes her vigilance to the extreme. When one of her kids goes to a sleepover, she wants to know exactly what he ate, what time he fell asleep, what he watched on television and how many times he said "please" and "thank you." She scolds her twelve-year-old for being two minutes late to breakfast and checks his homework to make sure that everything is perfectly completed.

Carol will likely run into problems as her children mature and require more emotional space to make decisions and exercise their individuality. A teenager in Carol's house is likely to become very angry and rebellious when faced with rigid requirements and rules. He may act out or adopt a passive-aggressive defense to cunningly prove that "Mom can't control me." Another child may respond to this kind of environment by becoming overly compliant, impeding his emotional maturity. While Carol so diligently controls the externals of parenthood, she often ignores the lessons wisdom has concerning the hearts and character of her children. Their development is lost in superficial checklists.

Controlling Carol's perspective and actions mirror those of the Pharisees in the New Testament. In their efforts to get everything just right, they completely missed the most important lessons. Their disdain for what they could not understand or control blinded their eyes to Jesus. Motherhood is filled with chaos. Although some structure is essential, we can see the face of wisdom most clearly when we let go of our need to control.

Fearful Fran

Several years ago, I was speaking at a homeschooling convention, and I met Fran. Close by her side was her son, an overweight, shy twelve-year-old. "I sent John to school through the first grade. I pulled him out because he got teased." John listened intently as his mother explained to me that he wasn't confident enough to go to youth group or any other activity with peers. "Kids can be so mean. I don't want him to have to face that."

You can probably understand the reality of Fran's fears for her son. You can probably also see how those fears kept her from wisely helping John develop confidence. Fran's fears had become John's fears. Without realizing it, she was communicating to him that he could not handle interacting with peers. Although she sought to protect him, she had actually handicapped him.

There are a lot of things to be afraid of with our kids— legitimate fears. Certainly we need to be aware of dangers and vigilant to avoid them. But our fears as mothers can be taken to an extreme, creating anxiety and dependence in our children. Finding the balance between trusting God with our children yet being careful is difficult. We want our kids to be aware of danger, but we don't want them to live in fear.

This balance can particularly be difficult to achieve for a mother who was not protected during her own childhood. Those who were victimized sexually, abused physically or verbally, or subjected to frightening environments as children may still feel unsafe as adults. Danger seems to lurk around every

Using technology to allay your child's fears.

Reprinted by permission of John McPherson, as appeared in Chicken Soup for the Soul Cartoons for Moms.

corner. Certainly a loving mother protects her child from every conceivable danger. Overcompensating with safety measures can be a functional way of coping with fears. However, overprotective moms often communicate to their children a lack of confidence in them.

Extreme fearfulness models and reinforces a lack of trust in God. Although a mother may not be able to eliminate her fearful feelings, she can decide how to respond to her fear. "Do not be anxious about anything, but in everything, by prayer and petition, with thanksgiving, present your requests to God. And the peace of God, which transcends all understanding, will guard your hearts and your minds in Christ Jesus" (Phil. 4:6–7).

Lonely Lynnette

My little boys are at such wonderful ages. They adore their mother. They each love to be cuddled and hugged. Right now, I am the most important person in their world. If my husband is out of town, any of the three would love to sleep in Mommy's bed or stay up late and watch cartoons with me. My three little buddies.

I've done enough family counseling to know that I won't always have such a fan club under my roof. The day will soon come when these boys would rather I not kiss them goodnight. In fact, they may find me downright embarrassing and repulsive in the future. When Michael was first born, I remember having the most surprising thought: *What if he doesn't like me?* If I listen to wisdom, there will surely be days when he and his brothers won't like me.

Every mother wants to be loved by her children, but this desire is overwhelming for Lynette. No matter what the cost, she must never let her children leave or reject her. Lynette may even subconsciously create financial or emotional dependence in her children so that they always need her. She makes decisions not centered on wisdom, but based on how they will affect her child's feelings towards her. Lynette may even alienate her child from others who are a threat to their affection for her, discouraging a romance or marriage, criticizing the child's father, or deterring friendships. The message Lynette wants her child to believe is, "I will always be the most important person in your life." Lynette probably considers herself a loving mother, and in many ways she is probably right. However, her own needs for companionship and love drive her maternal behavior.

Single mothers (or those in unfulfilling marriages) often have to resist the urge to become a Lynette. Because their emotional needs for an intimate relationship are not met by a husband, they naturally have some of these needs met by their children; their children are often happy to oblige. Being Mommy's "special friend" can be very rewarding for a child initially. However, it interferes with healthy emotional development and can become a significant burden for kids.

As I stated before, there is no "I" in motherhood. Although being a mom can be incredibly rewarding, our fulfillment has to come from pleasing God as mothers. We have genuine needs for significance, value, friendship, security and love. It's easy to lean on our kids to meet these needs without even knowing it. When we seek fulfillment through parenting, we can't listen to wisdom's cry. We feel too dependent to seek lasting changes. The freedom to listen to wisdom is only possible when our focus is on God; He is the One we depend on and strive to please. We have to consistently remind ourselves that parenting is a ministry, not a vehicle to fulfill our own needs. If we depend upon Him, God will equip us with what we lack!

Now that you know how to find wisdom, will you let yourself be changed by her? Reflect on these words of James:

> *Do not merely listen to the word, and so deceive yourselves. Do what it says. Anyone who listens to the word but does not do what it says is like a man who looks at his face in a mirror and, after looking at himself, goes away and immediately forgets what he looks like. But the man who looks intently into the perfect law that gives freedom, and continues to do this, not forgetting what he has heard, but doing it—he will be blessed in what he does.*
>
> (Jas. 1:22–25)

Do you really want to parent guilt-free? If so, then remember that trusting God is a daily commitment to changing according to His wisdom. At many times in motherhood, wisdom sounds too difficult, too painful and too time-consuming, which is precisely why so few people faithfully live by the life-giving principles that are available to everyone.

Oh, Lord, may we learn to hate our foolishness as much as we hate vomit!

For Personal Reflection

1. Take some time to honestly evaluate your response to wisdom's call. In what areas do you refuse to listen to wisdom?

_____

_____

2. Which of the caricatures do you most identify with? How does your need keep you rooted in foolishness?

_____

_____

3. How can you seek God's grace and sufficiency for your needs?

_____

_____

4. How have parenting successes made you confident in your own wisdom? How can you stay hungry for God's wisdom, even in the midst of success?

_____

_____

8

A Buffet of Guilt

Although all mothers at some level deal with inadequacy, certain issues and circumstances create tremendous feelings of guilt. In this chapter, we look briefly at a few of them: working outside the home, the past, single parenting, the influence of others, death or illness of a child, and significant personal limitations.

"WORKING" MOMS

Working outside of the home is a primary source of guilt for many mothers. Missing milestones, always seeming rushed and irritable, feeling like you are not bonding with your kids and perhaps even looking forward to escaping to work can heap on additional feelings of guilt. What's more, everyone has an opinion about whether you should or shouldn't be away from your kids.

"Do you work?" a man recently asked me after finding out that I am a mother of three. Only a man, right?

What kind of question is that? Of course I work. All mothers work. What makes work work? A paycheck? Leaving the house? A job description? Nowadays, the distinction of what constitutes a "working mother" is not always clear. Jobs come in every form and fashion. Creative moms are learning how to fit them into their ever-changing lifestyles. Some moms have outside jobs during the school year, but stay home in the summer. Other moms work from home. Still others spend fifteen hours a week in church meetings and volunteer work. Homeschooling moms work as teachers.

Even in the midst of all the flexibility and variables, the issue of working outside of the home continues to be a major source of guilt for moms. While working moms sometimes feel defensive about being away from their kids, stay-at-home moms can feel inadequate about not "doing it all." These two camps can be judgmental and critical of each other, heaping further guilt onto the issue.

"Should I work or stay home with my kids?" Perhaps answering this question spawns so much guilt because it's the wrong question. The answer places the responsibility squarely on Mom's shoulders. She may second-guess her decision daily. Guilt-free mothers, instead, should ask questions like, "God, what do you want me to do with this time?" "How can I use my

Reprinted by permission of John McPherson, as appeared in Chicken Soup for the Soul Cartoons for Moms.

abilities to serve you now?" and "How do you want me to care for these children?" Remember, these are not *our* children, and the hours are not *ours* to spend. We do our work, including motherhood, "heartily unto the Lord!" Ask God for direction and faithfully spend your days at whatever work He puts in front of you, at home or otherwise.

Whether or not you work outside of the home is not the issue. More importantly, why do you work outside the home or why do you stay home? You can stay home for all the wrong reasons or work for all the right reasons.

Your decisions of when to work, how much and where may need to be visited several times throughout motherhood. At certain ages, your children may need more of your physical and emotional attention. Your financial situation may change based on your husband's health or job.

God has gifted you with specific gifts and abilities. He has also entrusted you with the primary care of children. How you balance this responsibility at different stages of your life is between you and Him (and your husband). He knows your financial situation, your children's needs, the opportunities you have, your background and your dreams. Are you willing to seek Him and trust His direction? If He were to ask you to change your course, are you willing to do that? If so, then you have nothing to feel guilty about.

PAST MISTAKES

For some people, reading this book may create far more guilt than it alleviates. What do you do if you've wasted years of parenting apart from godly wisdom? You can't go back and change the mistakes you have made. You can't erase the impact those years had on your children.

If you have areas in your past that you are truly guilty for, you need to deal with them. The Bible tells us that God completely forgives the sin of our past and remembers them no more. But we must confess our sin and accept that Christ paid the penalty on the cross.

Although God may "forget" our sin, our memories are often more difficult to erase. Often we continue to feel guilty even after we have dealt with our sin before God. Forgiveness is so intangible, and the feelings of guilt are so poignant.

In the Old Testament, the Jewish people often built altars upon which they offered sacrifices for their sin. Jesus was the sacrifice on the cross that paid for all the sin of those who trust in Him. Although we no longer build sacrificial altars, it is still helpful to have tangible reminders of when we confess sin. Imagine if you could build an altar. Every time you felt guilty for a sin in the past, you would remind yourself, *I already dealt with that. The guilt I feel is false, because that account has been taken care of.*

Spend time pouring out your heart to God. Tell Him about the remorse you feel from the past. Confess your sin and trust God to make you "white as snow." The sacrifice the Lord wants from you is only a broken and contrite heart. Read Psalm 51. Then do something tangible to remind you of your confession and God's forgiveness. Journal, throw a stone into a lake or write a prayer. When feelings of guilt sneak up on you in the future, remember that your guilt has been dealt with!

As the apostle Paul states, "One thing I do: Forgetting what is behind and straining toward what is ahead, I press on toward the goal to win the prize for which God has called me heavenward in Christ Jesus" (Phil. 3:13–14). Paul certainly had a past to agonize over and feel guilty about. However, instead of wallowing in guilt, Paul used his errant background to praise God.

At various times in his writing he refers to his past, giving God the glory for his dramatic conversion from sinfulness. Paul acknowledges that his past is part of what God has used to make him effective in the future.

Remember also that God's work in your children's lives is not limited by your past failures. In fact, He can use those difficulties to form character in their lives. Your children can be just as influenced by the way you handle your past as they are by the past itself. Let them witness the difference God makes in your life. Let them see the freedom from sin and guilt that Christ purchased on the cross.

SINGLE PARENTING

Not a week goes by that I don't think, *How do single moms do it?* What an astounding task it must be to earn money, raise children and run a household by yourself! There is absolutely no way that a single parent can feel capable of doing a job that normally taxes the resources of two people. The resulting guilt can be crippling.

Take Kathy, a single mom of two boys. Her job in real estate provides enough to cover expenses and afford a few luxuries. Although she likes her job, she never feels free to enjoy it. When she is at work, she worries about her kids. Because she is rushing to get work done so she can be with her children, her boss sometimes complains about Kathy's lack of commitment to work. When Kathy is home, she is exhausted. Although she is physically with her children, she knows she is short-tempered and never has the energy to play with them. Who will teach her sons how to throw a football, how to confront a bully or how to romance a sweetheart? She feels so inadequate to the task. Every evening she falls into bed, completely spent, but also knowing that her efforts were woefully inadequate for what her children need. Many are the nights that she falls asleep with her pillow damp with her tears.

Compounding your feelings of inadequacy as a single parent may be your guilt from the past. Knowing that God designed children to be raised by a mother and father, you may feel responsible for placing yourself and your children in a single-parent situation. Perhaps you were not married when you got pregnant or your actions contributed to your divorce. Maybe you have never let go of anger and hatred toward your ex-husband. Managing the overwhelming job of the present is impossible if you carry around guilt from the past.

Far more crippling than a single-parent or blended-family household for your child may be your burden of guilt. Single moms sometimes respond to their guilt by overcompensating with unhealthy affection and expectations. The intense mother-child bond often overshadows the message of wisdom. Remember that you have to let go of what you are holding on to in order to grasp wisdom!

Once the past has been addressed, trust God for His sufficiency in your current circumstances. He is a God of new beginnings. He knows your limitations. Pray for His grace in your own life and in your children's lives. Ask Him to provide what you lack. Psalm 68:5–6 says, "A father of the fatherless, a defender of widows, is God in his holy dwelling. God sets the lonely in families." God's work may often be accomplished through His body. Remember that Christians all around the world are your new family! Don't be afraid to lean on them for companionship, wisdom and help.

God does not need ideal circumstances to accomplish His purpose in your children's life. He can even use the struggles of growing up in a single-parent family to develop sensitivity and dependence upon Him.

THE INFLUENCE OF OTHERS

Although mothers have tremendous influence with their children, so do other people. Peers, teachers, coaches and even Hollywood superstars have an increasing impact as children age. No mother can escape at least some frustration and anxiety resulting from how other people affect her children. It can seem as if other people are sabotaging all of your efforts. How can years of parental influence be erased by a few weeks of hanging out with a group of friends? Why does a pro football player have more influence over your son than you do?

You have the right and responsibility to know what is going on when others are with your children. Short of their father, you do not have to allow anyone to have access to your kids. Be vigilant and aware of how others treat your children. If you have any reservations, don't be afraid to put your foot down!

Sometimes a mom genuinely does not have the ability to shelter her children from the influence of others. This situation is often a concern of divorced mothers who have no control over the environment their children walk into during visitation.

Chris, a single mother, is tied up in knots at the thought of her thirteen-year-old son and ten-year-old daughter spending weekends with their dad. Nine years ago, her husband fell in love with another woman and demanded a divorce. Since then, Chris has devoted her life to helping her children recover from the trauma. She doesn't want them to ever feel responsible or unloved because of the divorce. She hates that she can't give them a traditional, functional family, but she is determined to make the best of it.

Chris's husband eventually married the other woman. Together, they have another child who is clearly the center of the home. Whenever Chris's children spend time with their father and his wife, they feel like second-class citizens. They are often berated and ridiculed by their stepmom, as they represent the ex-wife. Their father seems oblivious to their pain and often adds to it by his indifference. The children dread the regular visitation, but Chris understands that she legally cannot interfere.

Chris must clearly define her personal responsibility in this situation. She has a limited sphere of influence and cannot assume responsibility for what she can't control. Although her children's situation may cause her grief, she has to stay focused on maximizing her influence in their lives. She must remember that trying to control ultimately compromises influence.

Chris cannot control her ex-husband or his wife. She can make requests of them, but she cannot take responsibility for how they react to the kids. She is only responsible for how *she behaves* toward the children, their father and their stepmother. Although Chris cannot change the situation, she can be a godly influence within less than ideal circumstances.

> Worrying, manipulating and trying to control take away time, energy and focus from where we *can* make a difference.

Worrying, manipulating and trying to control take away time, energy and focus from where we *can* make a difference. We can be so upset about how others interact with our children that we completely neglect how *we* are supposed to love and teach them.

Jane was furious about how her husband interacted with their children. He had a terrible temper, and he was critical and sarcastic. Over the years, Jane defended her children to their father. She began giving him a taste of his own medicine, criticizing and humiliating him in front of the kids. By doing so, she completely compromised her own influence. She never intended to give her kids a model of a bitter and spiteful wife! She was only trying to undo her husband's damage.

The same is true of all of the people in your children's lives. You cannot control them. Although you cannot be responsible for the impact they have with your children, you can seek God's wisdom and grace as you deal with each individual. As tempting as it might be to become resentful toward someone who poses a threat, Scripture gives us clear guidelines for our own responsibility and behavior. Our responsibility is to do everything within our power to limit dangerous influences in our children's lives. Then we must be very prayerful and deliberate to neither assume responsibility for others nor to be destructive with our influence.

A mother, like Chris and Jane, who finds herself fretting and worrying about the uncontrollable influences in her children's lives may also find comfort in the fact that she can empower and encourage her children through difficulties. She may not be able to eliminate the bully at school or the critical stepmother, but she can teach her child coping strategies. She can apply words of comfort to painful wounds. Most importantly, she can pray fervently with and for her children. God sees every tear, knows each fear, and has the power to protect and reassure when a mother cannot.

DEALING WITH THE DEATH OR ILLNESS OF A CHILD

Jon and Marci had prayed for a child for so long. A few years ago they got pregnant, only to have a first-trimester miscarriage. Then, they got pregnant again. As the first trimester came and went, they breathed a sigh of relief. After years of watching their friends become parents, their turn had finally come. Everyone was so happy for them! Excitedly, she went to her first ultrasound. Today, they would find out if they were having a boy or a girl. They found out a lot more than that. Their baby's brain was not developing. They were told the pregnancy could go full term, but the baby would not survive outside the womb.

Jon and Marci were given a choice. They could terminate the pregnancy or carry their child, knowing that he would not live past birth. For five more months, Marci carried her son, Ty. As they grieved and questioned God's plan, they shared their journey with family and friends, journaling through e-mails. Marci's belly grew, and she felt Ty kick as the pregnancy progressed. Innocent strangers asked her the normal questions when they saw her protruding stomach: "When are you due?" "What are you having?" "I'll bet you're excited!"

As the ninth month approached, Jon and Marci didn't have a baby shower; they planned a funeral. Instead of painting a nursery, Jon made a casket. Ty James was born. Surrounded by family and friends, he lived for almost three hours. During that time, he was cuddled and loved and prayed for. Marci wore the proud smile of any mother. She beamed as she held her newborn son. . . . Then came the inevitable. Death.

Maybe you have experienced a loss like this. Certainly, you know someone who has. A baby dies of SIDS, a child dies of leukemia, a teenager dies in a car accident. We are left with questions that seem too big for answers.

Nothing in life could possibly be more difficult for a mother than losing a child. A mother may never stop grieving the death of her child. Birthdays uncelebrated, watching other children pass milestones that theirs never will, longing to see that face one more time.

How can the death of a child be anything but tragic? The parents of children who die often feel tremendously responsible. Sometimes they blame the death on their own negligence: a child fell down the stairs, drowned in the bathtub or was hit by a car. Even when no connection is obvious, they feel guilty for passing on a defective gene or not finding the right doctor.

No words are adequate to address the waves of grief and guilt these parents must feel. Within our limited understanding, we cannot fathom where God may be in such tragedy. Perhaps the only comfort comes in knowing that God is in control. Each one of our kids could have easily died many times. All it takes is the wrong mosquito bite, a bad hamburger, a swallowed nickel or an icy spot in the road. In His wisdom, God allows some to live and some to die. Short of murder, no parent is *responsible* for a child's death. Only the Lord numbers our days. Only by His grace do any of us take another breath.

How futile it is to cling to life! Whether three hours or eighty years, life is fleeting. Read the wisdom and perspective Moses gave us near the end of his life:

> *You turn men back to dust,*
> *   saying, "Return to dust, O sons of men."*
> *For a thousand years in your sight*
> *   are like a day that has just gone by,*
> *   or like a watch in the night. . . .*
>
> *The length of our days is seventy years—*
> *   or eighty, if we have the strength;*

> *yet their span is but trouble and sorrow,*
>   *for they quickly pass, and we fly away.*
>
> *Who knows the power of your anger?*
> *For your wrath is as great as the fear due you.*
> *Teach us to number our days aright,*
> *that we may gain a heart of wisdom.*

(Ps. 90:3–4; 10–12)

God's sovereignty doesn't mean our children will live long, healthy lives. But it does mean that God created them for a unique purpose. Their lives are not an accident, but part of God's divine plan. From the time they were within the womb, God knit them together to perfectly fulfill His plan for them!

The Bible gives us some great examples of God's wisdom and glory shining through tragic circumstances. The most obvious example is Job. When we read the story of Job, we always focus on the main character. But other lives played into the drama, his wife and friends among them. What about Job's ten children? All we know about them is that they were eating dinner together when a tornado caused the house to collapse. They all died. Were their deaths in vain?

How about David and Bathsheba's son? Because of their sin, "the LORD struck the child . . . and he became ill" (2 Sam. 12:15). It wasn't the baby's fault. Why did he die?

One of the most tragic circumstances is Jonathan's son, Mephibosheth. The boy was five years old when his father and grandfather (Saul) were killed in battle. "His nurse picked him up and fled, but as she hurried to leave, he fell and became crippled" (2 Sam. 4:4). When David became king, he adopted Mephibosheth out of kindness to Jonathan.

In each of these awful situations, God's purpose was established. Each child played a role in God's story to us. None of their parents would have chosen that particular role for their children. In their limited view, what happened was terrible. But God used tragedy and pain to be glorified. He also gave the grace to those who trusted him to persevere through adversity.

Jon and Marci's most difficult decision was not whether to carry their son to full term. More importantly, they had to decide whether to fight against God's sovereignty or lean into it. When people asked them how they were able to endure, they told them, "This is the baby we prayed for, and this is the baby that God has given us. We will love and care for him for as long as God allows." They demonstrated such confidence in God! Here is what Marci wrote briefly after her son died:

> *Through the five months of knowing our baby would die and wondering why it had to be that way, we made a decision to trust God's plan. This plan was not at all what our dreams pictured, but we held tight to God's promises. These promises that are so evident throughout the Bible spoke to us loudly, gave us peace and carried us along the way. My job as a mom would be short, but I vowed to do my absolute best at carrying my baby, planning and getting ready for his needs when he would be born, and most*

importantly praying that his life, as short as it would be, would glorify God.

As the time came, God beautifully orchestrated the night Ty was born. Because God is good, and because we trusted and surrendered the situation to him, we can say the night was perfect. God's plan for our son was right. I will never regret making the decision to jump on board with that plan and watch God carry us through an amazing ninth-month journey of parenthood. What a thrill to experience God's wisdom and strength in such a weak situation.

The difference between three hours and fifty years with our children is a lifetime to us, but a breath to God. His purposes were accomplished through Ty's brief life and through his parents' faithful testimony. Although their pain may be great, their joy is complete, knowing that God is working. Yes, their dreams went unfulfilled and their longings to hold Ty will not be satisfied on this side of heaven. But God is God, and He has been honored through what we understand as tragedy.

You can never lay your guilt down until you lean into God's sovereignty. It's okay to be angry, confused and bewildered. God can handle your emotions and questions. However, He may not give you the answers you seek. When Job questioned Him, God answered by reminding Him of His greatness. You can never understand His ways, but faith is trusting what you don't understand.

PERSONAL LIMITATIONS

Heather was thirty-two and the mother of three girls when she was diagnosed with bipolar disorder (manic depression). Throughout her young adulthood, she had struggled with mood swings. For weeks she would be so depressed that she could barely get out of bed. Other times, she would be irritable and unreasonable. She often felt like she couldn't control her own behavior. Worse than Heather's guilt about yesterday was the knowledge that she very well might repeat her offenses tomorrow. How could God have entrusted these children to her when she could barely function herself?

All mothers have limitations, but yours may be extreme. Mental illness, physical handicaps, terminal illness, addictions or extreme past trauma—many mothers struggle with such circumstances, which interfere with their capacity to care for their children.

If you have a significant limitation as a mom, first realize that you are parenting under unique circumstances. As much as you may hate to accept it, your approach to motherhood may need to differ from the norm. If you pretend that your limitation does not exist, you are parenting to prove a point, not to follow wisdom. Ultimately, your stubbornness or denial will hurt your children far more than your limitation ever could.

How humbling to admit the need for help! You look around at all the other moms who seem to manage quite well. You feel worthless and guilty that you can't be the mom you want to be for your kids. However, refusing to admit your need for help only makes the situation worse. Heather sometimes grew so frustrated at not being "normal" that she determined to outwit her disease. She quit taking her medication, stopped meeting with her doctor and applied all of her willpower to controlling her emotions. At these times she was the most ineffective as a mother. Only through accepting her disability could she seek the help to manage it.

Accepting a disability may also mean that you need help caring for your children. A mother with chronic fatigue syndrome can't carpool all over creation, host a sleepover, clean her house and make gourmet meals. She must rely on relatives, friends or paid help to care for her family.

Remember that God has not asked you to be all things to your children. He only expects you to be faithful with the resources He has given you. You can still manage the care of your children even if you can't physically or emotionally do all the work yourself.

If you have experienced one of these "courses" in the buffet of guilt, feelings of worthlessness and inadequacy likely haunt you. When they do, remember Paul's words of wisdom in Hebrews 12:1–2:

> "...let us throw off everything that hinders and the sin that so easily entangles, and let us run with perseverance to race marked out for us. Let us fix our eyes on Jesus, the author and pertruder of our faith ..."

Acquitting the guilt and condemning the innocent—the Lord detests them both.

Proverbs 17:15

For Personal Reflection

1. How has the area of outside work added to your feelings of guilt or inadequacy?

_____

_____

2. What events from the past do you feel guilty about? Have you dealt with this issue before God? If so, when? If not, what's getting in your way?

_____

_____

3. What limitations do you have as a mother? Do you mask these limitations or ask for help?

_____

_____

4. What relationships in your children's lives are you concerned about? What can you do with your influence to impact these relationships? In what ways is your influence limited?

_____

_____

5. Do you really believe that God can be glorified through your children, even if the circumstances are less than ideal? How does this belief impact the way you parent?

_____

_____

9

Good-Bye, Guilt

There once was a young man who was taken into captivity as a prisoner of war. He was imprisoned in a cell in the middle of the desert. Every day, the desert winds blew great quantities of sand into his cell. If he failed to shovel out the sand, within days his cell would be overtaken with it and he would die. The young man went through periods of depression, during which he would let the sand build up almost to the point of suffocation. He was overwhelmed with the futility of his life, shoveling for another day of survival. At other times, his task became a challenge. He worked laboriously thinking of faster and easier ways of shoveling.

After fifteen years of captivity, his liberators came. The door of his cell opened and he was free—free from shoveling, free from sand, free from meaninglessness. At first he was filled with excitement at the promise of a full life. But as he emerged from his cell and felt the strong rays of the sun, his heart was gripped with fear. Shoveling the sand had become his life—his fight for survival. He had become good at it. Why would he leave the only world he had known and mastered? The man chose to stay in his cell, content to shovel the sand.

Several years ago, a colleague told me this story. She found such hope in it—that the routine things of life could become meaningful. She concluded that our task in life is to master the mundane. To me, the story spoke of another profound truth: We can become so comfortable in our bondage that we fail to embrace the freedom that Christ offers.

As a mom, your motherhood can sometimes feel like the prisoner in the story, as if each day you wake up to shovel a mountain of sand before it overwhelms you. The "sand" is more than the obvious laundry, dirty dishes and to-do lists. The true "shoveling" occurs in our minds: *Does the good outweigh the bad I've done? How can I compensate for the mistakes I've made as a mom?* And no matter how proficient you become at shoveling that sand, it never stops blowing in. As long as you are breathing, you still face both your deliberate sin and your accidental failures as a mother.

Christ offers freedom from the futility of a life spent shoveling. But accepting it requires that you walk away from what has grown comforting, perhaps the only way you know how to parent. It means stepping into the unknown.

We deal with guilt so much because we live daily with the

direct impact we have on our children. Our words can make them laugh or cry, our actions can make them feel loved or rejected. We want to influence them so perfectly—an impossible task. We hope and pray that our efforts will be enough, anxiously waiting to see the results of our parenting.

The whole picture of godly wisdom suggests a drastically different approach to motherhood that can be, indeed, guilt-free. According to God's word, the ultimate goal in parenting is not to raise good children, although this is often the byproduct. Your motherhood should not necessarily be judged by the final result. Your guilt or innocence has

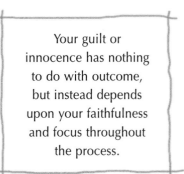

Your guilt or innocence has nothing to do with outcome, but instead depends upon your faithfulness and focus throughout the process.

nothing to do with outcome, but instead depends upon your faithfulness and focus throughout the process.

What if motherhood has as much to do with your maturity as it does with your child's? You may focus so much on what you think God wants to do with your children that you neglect what He wants to do with *you*. You, also, are *His* child. As you build your children, so is He building you. Through asking you to accomplish the impossible task of motherhood, He is not setting you up for guilt-inducing failure, but the potential for faith-producing maturity.

God cares deeply about your children, even more than you do. But He also wants the process of motherhood to radically change you. He wants each fear and failure to drive you closer to dependence upon Him. He wants each challenge to make you hungry for His wisdom, and each unknown to strengthen your faith.

In many ways, guilt-free motherhood is difficult. No formula guarantees success, nor can you gloss over the seriousness of mistakes. You need to confront your selfishness, pride, fear and inadequacy. However, you can be freed from a burden that you were never meant to carry. God intends for you to be fully and faithfully invested in the process, not to be driven to control the result. Among all the many variables of motherhood, being truly guilt free depends upon only one: walking with God through the process.

As mothers, we often think of our children as the sole benefactor of our motherhood. Love, discipline, encouragement, servanthood: We do it all for our kids. Although everything we do as mothers involves our children, they should not be the primary reason for our actions.

Motherhood is just one aspect of your pilgrimage in serving God on this earth. Although it is a powerful and consuming commission, motherhood was never intended to overshadow your relationship with God. God has given you children so that you can express your faithfulness and love to Him. Your children must never replace God as the defining factor or vessel of hope in your life.

I absolutely believe that guilt-free motherhood is not only possible, but it is God's design for motherhood. I say this as a young mother who, like you, does not know the final result of my own parenting. But I do know, based on His word, what God has called me to do. I know what He requires from me as a mother, and I know that He has promised to equip me as I depend upon Him to fulfill this mission.

GUILT-FREE MOTHERHOOD IS ONLY POSSIBLE THROUGH THE CROSS

If we claim to be without sin, we deceive ourselves and the truth is not in us. If we confess our sin, he is faithful and just and will forgive us our sins and purify us from all unrighteousness.

(1 John 1:8–9)

Joanne loved being a mother. Having come from an abusive family, she was absolutely determined to provide a nurturing environment for her five children. Her husband owned his own business and was seldom home, so Joanne largely determined the tone of the household. She read books and listened to all the wisdom she could get on the topic of motherhood. She stayed up late and woke up early, pouring all of her thoughts, energy and love into her children.

When the fifth child was only a baby, Joanne's marriage began to crumble. She was absolutely spent! Everything she had hoped for and dreamed of was turning into a nightmare. How could her best efforts end up so short?

Separated and on the way to divorce, Joanne began to seek God. Raised as a nominal Catholic, her faith had never gone beyond occasionally going to Mass. "Lord, I have given all that

I know to give, and it isn't enough. Please, if you're out there, help me!" Throughout the next few months, Joanne and her husband began going to church together and truly seeking God. They learned what it was to genuinely have a relationship with God. Joanne started to realize why Jesus died on the cross and what it meant to serve Him as Lord. She began devoting her energy not to parenting perfectly, but to parenting as unto the Lord.

Your journey of guilt-free motherhood must begin at the cross. If you trust your own abilities and efforts to parent well, you will come up short. Even if your children turn out "okay," you will have missed out on God's entire purpose for your life: fellowshipping with Him and bringing Him glory.

In 1 Corinthians 1:30, we learn that *Christ became our wisdom.* Colossians 2:2 says that in Christ are hidden all the treasures of wisdom and knowledge. Only He is our confidence. Only in Him can we boast. Even though wisdom may help us "live well," it will ultimately mean nothing without completely depending upon Christ's work on the cross.

We are sinners. We have harmed our children already by our selfishness, pride and possessiveness. Although we cannot parent perfectly, admitting guilt is difficult. Ironically, we tend to *feel* guilty and ruminate over stupid mistakes and gloss right over the heart of our guilt: the guilt of our hearts!

Jesus said that all the commandments could be summed up with two: Love the Lord your God with all your heart, soul and strength, and love your neighbor as yourself. When we use that measure to evaluate our attitudes as moms, we recognize how greatly we need the cross.

Even the good things we do for our children are so often motivated out of our own desire to feel good, to be loved or to feel successful. When we subtly brag about our children's abilities or success, when we doubt God's protection and plan for them, when we demand their love and attention, when we teach them to depend upon us and not God, these are the sins we rarely feel guilty about because we don't see them as sin. But they are! Pride, anxiety, the sense of ownership and entitlement with our children all speak of our true guilt. They are the sinful attitudes that keep from us wholly trusting in God.

The greatest of all our sin is our desire to be perfect. We want to be God; we don't want to have to trust Him. Isn't this the very sin that tripped up Lucifer and Eve? These may not be "juicy sins," but they keep us and our children from knowing God's power in our lives. They place the burden of parenthood squarely on our independent shoulders.

Do you realize how guilty you are of sin? Not just the obvious sin, but the subtle sins of rebellion? Do you also realize what Christ's blood means to that sin? When we confess, He is faithful and just to cleanse us. It's done! Guilt is gone! It means placing all responsibility for the results clearly on His shoulders from this day forward. It means resigning our role of commander-in-chief and embracing servanthood to Christ. We are mothers in His service doing His bidding. Strictly ambassadors.

GUILT-FREE MOTHERHOOD IS
ONLY POSSIBLE ABIDING IN CHRIST

I am the vine; you are the branches. If a man remains in me and I in him, he will bear much fruit; apart from me you can do nothing.

(John 15:5)

"From the time I wake up until the time I fall asleep at night, every moment seems to be spent. Parenting doesn't feel like a very spiritual task. There were times earlier in my life when I loved to spend time with God. Now that seems impossible as a mother of four teenagers!"

At a mothers' group, we were talking about the importance of prayer and reading the Bible. As the discussion deepened, so did the discomfort of many of the moms in the group. No one doubted their need to spend time with God. But let's face it: spiritual growth rarely outranks cooking, carpooling, sleeping and personal hygiene on the priority list. When was the last time you chose to delve into the Bible instead of vegging in front of the television after a long, draining day? Talk about guilt!

Why is time spent with God so important to motherhood? Isn't it just another one of those things we "should do"—like cleaning out the Tupperware closet or flossing our teeth—but never get to?

We don't have to spend hours a day on our knees or in the Bible to abide in Christ. But we must make fellowship with Him a priority. We are made with rechargeable spiritual batteries. Getting charged up at church once a week isn't enough to fight our human urges to take control and parent out of our own efforts. David, in Psalm 1, talks about being like a tree, planted right by the source of water. The disciplines of prayer and time with God remind us that we must be planted right by the source of our strength. Daily we must meditate on Him and talk to Him. Our time with God reminds us of the biblical perspective of guilt-free motherhood.

We can do a lot of physical and emotional things for our children apart from Christ. But there is nothing, absolutely nothing, we can do to save them or love them completely. When we parent apart from Christ, we feel guilty and inadequate. We fail. Our own reasoning and wisdom falls far short.

Guilt-free motherhood means parenting from the perspective of working alongside what God is doing. He is the craftsman, and we are the instrument in His hand, which means abiding in Him, seeking Him and knowing Him.

> *Like newborn babies, crave pure spiritual milk, so that by it you may grow up in your salvation.*
>
> (1 Pet. 2:2)

You cannot will yourself to be a godly mother. By sheer effort, you cannot achieve guilt-free motherhood. Guilt-free motherhood is the by-product of seeking God. The fruits of godliness are only possible by craving God and His word as a baby cries for milk. It's not about effort; it's about surrendering.

The Word of God is filled with wisdom. Throughout this book you have studied God's promise to give you His wisdom when you ask for it, when you hunger for it. He will equip you for this task if you seek His face! Wisdom is your daily bread, sustaining you through the challenges of motherhood.

GUILT-FREE MOTHERHOOD IS ONLY POSSIBLE IN IMPERFECTION

I wrote this book out of weakness. I didn't choose the topic of guilt-free motherhood because I had mastered it. I chose it out of my own struggle to find security in the shifting sands of motherhood. As a psychologist, I am privy to many people who have been wounded, often unknowingly, by their mothers. I also meet with women who carry tremendous guilt and regret because of mistakes they have made with their children. As I began to recognize my own fear and guilt, I wanted to find my confidence in Christ as I parent my children.

God used my weakness to draw me and others to Him. He can't be glorified in my strength. I don't need to trust Him in areas in which I feel strong. Only in my weakness can I point others to the power of Christ.

There are times when we feel weak and inadequate as mothers. But read what the Apostle Paul wrote about his weakness:

> *Three times I pleaded with the Lord to take it away from*
> *me. But he said to me, "My grace is sufficient for you, for*

my power is made perfect in weakness." Therefore I will boast all the more gladly about my weaknesses, so that Christ's power may rest on me. That is why, for Christ's sake, I delight in weaknesses. . . . For when I am weak, then I am strong.

(2 Cor. 12:8–10)

Imagine that! The things that you worry about the most—your weaknesses—are where Christ can work the most. Talk about guilt-free! Boast in your weakness, pointing to your all-powerful heavenly Father who can do anything! Remember, if you had no weaknesses, your children would never seek God. Only through your limitations as a mother can you direct your child's attention to an unfailing Savior.

Satan loves to glory in our weakness for a different purpose. He teases us with them, convincing us how inadequate we are to serve God. He reminds us to try harder within our flesh—to demand perfection. Like he did with Eve, he tempts us to chase after god-like wisdom and perfection. But God says that He has chosen the foolish and the base things of the world to confound the wise. He wants to be glorified in our weakness so that we, our children and everyone else can know that He alone deserves the praise.

Remember that Satan can use the "good" to overshadow the "great." From an earthly perspective, striving for perfection as a mother is a noble endeavor. In God's economy, it's a treadmill that wastes energy going nowhere. He didn't make you to be perfect; He made you to be needy!

One day, you will not only complete motherhood, you will pass from this life. From God's standpoint, the time is short and the end is near. You will soon take your last breath and enter the presence of God. The intimacy of the moment, looking into the eyes of Christ, will be overwhelming! So much of what you did during your lifetime will seem irrelevant: the piano lessons, cooking Thanksgiving dinner, folding laundry, carpooling. So few of the things that you worried about will matter. But will you be found faithful—not perfect—with the influence that God gave you? Will you have used the ministry of motherhood to wholeheartedly surrender your will to the Lord's? This, my dear friend, is the essence of guilt-free motherhood.

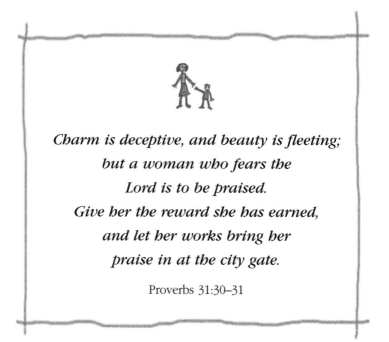

Charm is deceptive, and beauty is fleeting;
but a woman who fears the
Lord is to be praised.
Give her the reward she has earned,
and let her works bring her
praise in at the city gate.

Proverbs 31:30–31

For Personal Reflection

1. How is God working on your heart and teaching you as you teach your children?

_____

_____

2. What keeps you from daily drinking from God's Word? How does your time with God impact your ability to be guilt-free as a mother?

_____

_____

3. What are a few of your personal weaknesses that you believe interfere with your parenting? How can God be glorified through those weaknesses?

_____

_____

4. How has reading this book impacted the guilt you experience as a mother?

_____

_____

STUDY GUIDE

This twelve-week study guide is designed to be used both for personal and group formats. You will notice that each week is divided into three sections along with a fourth section, found at the end of each chapter in the book:

What Do You Think?

These questions are designed to promote generic group discussion about the material in the unit. They are nonthreatening but should prompt significant dialogue.

Digging for Wisdom

These questions are designed to point you to biblical material related to the topic at hand. They are ideal for personal devotions or group Bible study.

Taking It Home

This is a practical question or activity to help the reader apply the information learned.

For Personal Reflection

These questions, found at the end of each chapter, are designed to apply the material personally. Although they can be used in intimate group settings, their personal nature may be intimidating to share with unfamiliar people.

When planning a group study, use any combination of these questions to fit the make-up and purpose of the group. For example, a Bible study group that has been meeting for several years will probably want the challenge of "Personal Reflection" and "Digging for Wisdom" material. A newly formed neighborhood group might be more comfortable with "What do you think?" questions.

Week 1—Read Intro and Chapter 1

What Do You Think?

1. Guilt and motherhood seem to go hand in hand. Why is guilt a universal problem for moms? Why don't dads feel the same guilt?

_____

_____

2. Why do moms often feel like they have to be perfect? How does comparing notes with other moms play into maternal guilt?

_____

_____

3. What is the difference between the fact of being guilty and feelings of guilt? By what standard should we measure whether or not we are guilty?

_____

_____

4. How can guilty feelings be a form of self-punishment and atoning for wrongs? Give some examples.

_____

_____

5. Do you believe "Guilt-Free Motherhood" is possible? Why or why not?

_____

_____

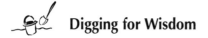 **Digging for Wisdom**

1. Read John 5:24, Romans 3:23–24, and Romans 5:6–11. What does Jesus' death on the cross mean for those who trust in Him for forgiveness?

_____

_____

2. Read Romans 8:1–17 and II Corinthians 7:9–11. What is the difference between the guilt of an unbeliever and the godly sorrow of a believer?

_____

_____

3. Read Micah 6:8, Proverbs 3:5–6, Psalm 37:3–9, I Corinthians 15:58 and Colossians 3:23. If Christ has taken away our guilt and punishment, we have no reason to feel guilty. We parent not to avoid punishment or to achieve perfection. So, what should be our focus and motivation in motherhood?

_____

_____

4. There are three causes of guilty feelings: our sin, our weakness and false guilt. What should be our response to each of these three?

     —Sin (Hebrews 10:15–23 and 12:1–11, James 4:7–10, I John 1:8–2:2)

     —Weakness (Isaiah 40:27–31, II Corinthians 12:7–10)

—False guilt (I Corinthians 4:3–5, Galatians 2:17–21 and 6:9)

_____

_____

 **Taking It Home**

This week, be aware of times when you feel guilty or fearful as a mom. How do these feelings impact your parenting?

_____

_____

WEEK 2—READ CHAPTER 2

What Do You Think?

1. Why is reactive parenting the enemy of effective motherhood?

   _____

   _____

2. Why do guilty feelings tend to make us more reactive? How does reactive parenting ultimately create more guilt?

   _____

   _____

3. What is the danger of being too busy as a mom? (Read Luke 10:38–42)

   _____

   _____

4. What is the difference between meeting your children's needs and giving in to their demands?

   _____

   _____

5. What is the difference between seeking wise advice and parenting by polling?

   _____

   _____

6. How do our own childhoods impact motherhood? Are we destined to repeat our parents' mistakes?

_____

_____

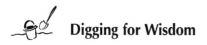 **Digging for Wisdom**

Although not a "parent," Jesus had twelve disciples and a multitude of followers. What pressures do you think He felt that might have tempted Him to be reactive?

1. Read Mark 2:15–3:6, 3:20–21, 3:31–35. What did the Pharisees think of Jesus' "parenting"? Who else was critical of Him? Why didn't He listen to their opinions?

_____

_____

2. Read Matthew 14:13–14, Mark 3:5–6, and John 2:13–17, 11:17–44. How did Jesus' emotions impact His actions?

_____

_____

3. Read Luke 5:16, 6:12 and 22:39–46. What did Jesus continually do to keep His focus? Why was it so important for Him to resist the pull to be reactive?

_____

_____

4. Read Matthew 7:7–11, James 4:2–6, and I John 3:21–22. How does God respond to the needs and demands of His children?

_____

_____

5. Read Proverbs 4:23–27 and Hebrews 12:1–2. How can we avoid being reactive?

_____

_____

 **Taking It Home**

Of the ones discussed, what do you tend to react to the most as a mother? What are three specific steps you can take to resist parenting reactively?

_____

_____

WEEK 3—READ CHAPTER 3

What Do You Think?

1. How will building a blueprint keep you from parenting reactively?

_____

_____

2. Our culture places a lot of emphasis on intelligence and education but very little on wisdom. What is the difference between being smart and being wise?

_____

_____

3. Why is "love not enough" for guilt-free motherhood?

_____

_____

4. How can studying the laws of God's creation make us wise? Share examples from your own parenting observations.

_____

_____

5. Why does wisdom seem so hard to find if it is crying out for us?

_____

_____

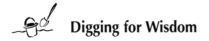

Digging for Wisdom

1. Read Solomon's prayer for wisdom in I Kings 3:7–9. What was his motivation for asking for wisdom? What was his heart attitude?

_____

_____

2. Read Colossians 3:16, Psalm 119:105 and Hebrews 4:12. Why is reading the Bible so essential for gaining wisdom? When has biblical wisdom helped you as a mother?

_____

_____

3. Read Proverbs 23:19, 22:15 and 29:15. How can we teach our children to love wisdom?

_____

_____

Taking It Home

God promises to give us wisdom when we ask for it. Write a prayer for wisdom, telling God about your fears and hopes as a mother.

_____

_____

WEEK 4—READ CHAPTER 4

What Do You Think?

1. What do you think of when you hear the phrase, "Fear the Lord"?

   _____

   _____

2. How is fearing God related to wisdom?

   _____

   _____

3. What is our culture's attitude toward fearing God? Give some examples.

   _____

   _____

4. Why is a parent's authority ultimately rooted in the fear of the Lord?

   _____

   _____

5. Do God's judgment and mercy compete with each other? How about a parent's love and discipline? Discuss the struggle to achieve this balance in motherhood.

   _____

   _____

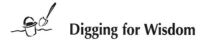 **Digging for Wisdom**

1. Does God really want His children to be afraid of Him? Read Psalm 25:14, Isaiah 8:13, Luke 12:7, I John 4:18, I Peter 1:17–19 and Proverbs 29:25. _____

_____

2. Read Proverbs 3:7, 8:13, 22:4 and Romans 11:20. How does fearing God relate to humility before the Lord?

_____

_____

3. Read Deuteronomy 5:11 and 28:58–59. Why do you think God makes such a big deal about the misuse of His name? How can you teach your children to show reverence for God's name? _____

_____

4. Read Proverbs 19:18, 22:6, 23:13–14, 29:15–17. How does consistent, loving discipline help our children? How does it relate to fearing the Lord? _____

_____

Taking It Home

What is one parenting change you want to focus on to impress upon your children the fear of the Lord?

_____

_____

WEEK 5—READ CHAPTER 5

What Do You Think?

1. Why is having "purpose" so important to motherhood?

_____

_____

2. How can a parent use wealth to teach productivity rather than indulging children? Why is this so difficult to do?

_____

_____

3. Why do you think kids who work hard grow up to be better adjusted adults?

_____

_____

4. Were you surprised by the results of "America's Report Card"? Why do you think integrity has become such a rarity among youth? Why do you think the study found no difference in children who were raised in religious households?

_____

_____

5. Why is integrity often viewed as the enemy of productivity? Cite some recent examples from your life in which you or your children had to choose between success and integrity.

_____

_____

Digging for Wisdom

1. Read Matthew 6:19–21, 24 and Mark 10:17–25. What warnings do these verses give about wealth? How are these warnings relevant to teaching productivity?

_____

_____

2. Read I Corinthians 15:58, II Thessalonians 3:10–13 and Matthew 25. How do we teach children about the importance of working hard and stewardship without teaching them to love money?

_____

_____

3. Read Joshua 1:6–9, Proverbs 16:3, Revelation 3:17–21, and Luke 16:1–12. How does God define success? How is His definition different than the world's?

_____

_____

4. Read Proverbs 6:16–19, 11:1, and 12:22. Why is punishing even little pockets of dishonesty so important to teaching integrity?

_____

_____

Taking It Home

Think of one practical way of emphasizing both productivity and integrity this week.

_____

_____

WEEK 6—READ CHAPTER 5

What Do You Think?

1. Why is training the tongue a central aspect of parenting?

   _____

   _____

2. Share some practical ways of teaching kids not to lie, sass, swear, tease and gossip and practical ways to encourage children to use their tongues positively.

   _____

   _____

3. Why is it so important for kids to have their own friends? Why are children often sensitive to their parent's criticism of their friends? _____

   _____

4. How can you make your home "kid-friendly"?

   _____

   _____

5. Why does Solomon emphasize the importance of accepting feedback to becoming wise?

   _____

   _____

6. Why is a foundation of love so important to giving feedback?

   _____

   _____

Digging for Wisdom

1. Read James 3:2 and Matthew 12:34–37. Why is restrained speech a hallmark of maturity?

   _____

   _____

2. Read James 3:13–18. James concludes his discussion of taming the tongue with some thoughts on wisdom. What does wisdom have to do with restrained speech?

   _____

   _____

3. Read Ephesians 4:17–5:21. Paul writes to the Ephesians about how to treat each other within the family of God. List at least six principles from this passage that apply to how we should use our tongues toward each other.

   _____

   _____

4. Read Psalm 1:1, Proverbs 16:28, 17:17–19, 18:24, 27:5–6 and 10, I Samuel 18:1–4 and 23:16–18. What qualities define a good friend? How can you teach your children to look for these in friends?

   _____

   _____

5. Read Nehemiah 9:13–31. How does God respond to us when we stubbornly refuse instruction? How can you

respond to a child who is closed to feedback or correction?

_____

_____

Taking It Home

Which of the three areas discussed this week (restrained speech, positive relationships and openness to feedback) is the most difficult for you? Pick one practical way to emphasize that aspect of wisdom in your parenting.

_____

_____

WEEK 7—READ CHAPTER 5

What Do You Think?

1. Why is self-control an important benchmark of maturity?

_____

_____

2. How can you teach your children to express anger appropriately and constructively? Give some examples.

_____

_____

3. What are your concerns about raising children in this sexually explicit climate? How can you prepare them to exercise self-control in this area?

_____

_____

4. A case can be made that contentment is the antidote to almost every sin. In Philippians 4:11–13, Paul shares that he has learned to be content in any circumstance by depending on God's strength. How can you teach your children the beauty of contentment?

_____

_____

5. How is each of the other six traits dependent upon "eye to the future"? _____

_____

6. How do you approach the balance between living for the future and enjoying the blessings of today?

_____

_____

 **Digging for Wisdom**

1. Read II Peter 1:3–11. How is self-control related to spiritual growth? How can you cultivate this fruit in your own life and your children's lives?

_____

_____

2. Read Genesis 4:6–7, Psalm 4:4, and Ephesians 4:26–27. What do these verses tell us about anger? Is it a sin? When does it become sinful?

_____

_____

3. Read Matthew 6:25–34. What is the difference between planning for tomorrow and worrying about it? How can you teach your children this difference?

_____

_____

4. Read Proverbs 3:21–26 and 4:25–27. How can you help a young child begin to think about future and eternal consequences? _____

_____

Taking It Home

Write down an age-appropriate area for each of your children in which they can exercise the muscle of self-control.

_____

_____

WEEK 8—READ CHAPTER 6

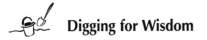 **What Do You Think?**

1. What is the difference between influence and control?

_____

_____

2. How does grasping for control compromise your influence?

_____

_____

3. What is a power struggle? What message about a child's free will does a power struggle communicate? Why is giving choices with consequences a wiser way to parent?

_____

_____

4. How does short-cutting consequences undermine moral development? When are you tempted to do this?

_____

_____

Digging for Wisdom

1. Read Genesis 2:15–17, 3:22–24 and Romans 5:12–19. How did God approach Adam's free will? Although He is the perfect parent, what did His child choose? What were the consequences? Although the consequences of Adam's

sin are permanent, what "second choice" did God give to Adam and to us?

_____

_____

2. Read the account of the prodigal son in Luke 15:11–32. How did the father avoid a power struggle with his son? What must it have felt like to see his son make a foolish choice? How did the father's respect for his son's free will encourage the son's moral development? Relate this example to a recent incident in your parenting.

_____

_____

3. Read Proverbs 2:1–11 and Ecclesiastes 1:12–18. These passages seem to contradict each other. If wisdom is "futile" why should we seek it? Where is the balance between seeking wisdom as mothers, yet acknowledging wisdom's limits?

_____

_____

Taking It Home

Think of an area in your children's lives in which you would like to eliminate their free will. How can you use your influence in this area without trying to control?

_____

_____

WEEK 9—READ CHAPTER 6

What Do You Think?

1. If you could "script" your children's lives, what would you plan for them?

   _____

   _____

2. Why is it difficult to trust that God's plan for our children is "good"? In your gut, do you trust His plan or yours? Why?

   _____

   _____

3. In what areas is it difficult to let go of your children? How might you justify holding on too tightly? How might your tendency to hold on interfere with your children's growth and maturity?

   _____

   _____

4. Why might maternal goals like "raising well-adjusted kids" or "putting my kids through college" be unhealthy and guilt-inducing? What kind of goals should replace these?

   _____

   _____

5. Why is praying for your children a vital discipline for motherhood? How does it encourage you to recognize God's ultimate control in their lives?

_____

_____

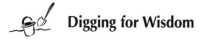 **Digging for Wisdom**

1. Read Jeremiah 17:5–9, Psalm 22:3–11, 40:4–5, and Proverbs 3:5–6. What is the difference between parenting based on our plan and placing our trust fully in God?

_____

_____

2. Read Jeremiah 10:23, Psalm 127:1–2, Proverbs 16:9, 19:21 and Matthew 6:25–34. Why is it futile for us to try to control our children's lives?

_____

_____

3. Read Exodus 32:9–14, Job 1:4–5, I Timothy 2:1 and James 5:16–20. There is a spiritual battle being waged for the souls of our children. What is the significance of your prayers for them?

_____

_____

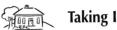 **Taking It Home**

In what areas is God asking you to loosen your grip on your children? Write a prayer to God acknowledging His sovereignty, your fears, and asking for His help to trust Him with the lives of your children.

_____

_____

Week 10—Read Chapter 7

What Do You Think?

1. What is the difference between being naive and being foolish? Why is foolishness like a dog returning to its vomit?

_____

_____

2. What do you think of the caricatures presented in the chapter? Why are a mother's needs so easily projected onto the job of parenting?

_____

_____

3. How can needs keep you from embracing wisdom?

_____

_____

4. Read Proverbs 1:20–33. What will happen to the fools and the naive who do not listen to wisdom? What do these warnings mean to you as a mother?

_____

_____

5. Solomon's life disproves the old adage: "with age comes wisdom." If Solomon can fall away from wisdom, so can any of us. How might the success wisdom brings be a

temptation for you to someday abandon her? Give some examples.

_____

_____

Digging for Wisdom

1. With all the wisdom Solomon left to us, the greatest warning comes from his own life. Read I Kings 9:1–9 and 11:1–13. Which principles of wisdom, from his own pen, did Solomon disregard?

Fear of the Lord	Openness to Feedback
Productivity	Self-Control
Uncompromising Integrity	Eye to the Future
Positive Relationships	

   _____

   _____

2. Read I Chronicles 28:9–10 and 29:10–20. What heritage and charge did David leave to his young son Solomon? Now read I Kings 11:29–43. What heritage did Solomon leave to his sons? David sinned too. Why did God continue to honor David in spite of his sin, yet we see no such restoration at the end of Solomon's life?

   _____

   _____

3. Assuming Solomon wrote Ecclesiastes at the end of his life, how do you think the events of his old age impacted the advice he gives about the limits of wisdom and the vanity of human wisdom and success?

_____

_____

Taking It Home

What do you need from God to stay open to and committed to godly wisdom? Write an honest prayer expressing your fears, desires and needs to Him.

_____

_____

Week 11—Read Chapter 8

What Do You Think?

1. In chapter 8, the author suggests that asking, "Should I work?" may be the wrong place to begin. Why is this the wrong question to ask? Discuss how decisions about work can be made from a perspective of godly wisdom.

   _____

   _____

2. How can mistakes and sins from years ago still impact a mother's ability to parent today? Can she ever be truly free from the guilt?

   _____

   _____

3. Why is it helpful to have a tangible reminder of when sin was confessed before God?

   _____

   _____

4. Talk about what it is like to be a single mother. What should be the responsibility of the body of Christ to single moms and their children?

   _____

   _____

5. Discuss some influences that you are concerned about regarding your children. How can you use your influence wisely in these situations?

_____

_____

6. How can God use tragedies or negative events in your life (or your child's life) for His glory? How do you feel about this?

_____

_____

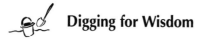 **Digging for Wisdom**

1. Read Philippians chapter 3. What in Paul's past did he have to feel guilty about? From his writing, does it seem that he had trouble forgiving himself? How did he turn his guilt into passion for Christ?

_____

_____

2. Read Psalm 139. Do you think these words are true about God's relationship to you? To your children? Do you live as though they are true?

_____

_____

3. Read Job 38, 39, 40:1–5 and Romans 9:10–24. When we doubt God's plan for our children's lives, what answer does God give us? How does this bring us back to lesson #1 of wisdom—the fear of the Lord?

_____

_____

 **Taking It Home**

Choose one course in the "buffet of guilt." What is one biblical concept you can focus on this week to become guilt-free in this area?

_____

_____

WEEK 12—READ CHAPTER 9

What Do You Think?

1. What comfort is there in parenting the way you always have? How does guilt-free motherhood depend upon stepping out of your comfort zone?

   _____

   _____

2. Why is guilt-free motherhood impossible without an acceptance of Jesus' death on the cross?

   _____

   _____

3. How can weakness be a way of teaching your children dependence upon Christ?

   _____

   _____

4. How can the "good overshadow the great" in motherhood?

   _____

   _____

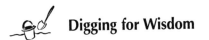 **Digging for Wisdom**

1. Read Psalm 1. Contrast the tree planted by the stream and the chaff that the wind blows away. Why is being in the Word of God so important to being rooted in godly wisdom?

   _____

   _____

2. Read I Corinthians 1:25–31, II Corinthians 7:10, Romans 8:26–39 and Isaiah 40:26–31. How do you think God feels about your weaknesses? How can He use them to be glorified and to bring you to childlike faith in Him?

   _____

   _____

 **Taking It Home**

What are three significant changes prompted by the study of _Guilt-Free Motherhood_ that you want to commit to as a mother? Write a prayer to God expressing your desire for Him to be glorified through you as you parent.

_____

_____

ABOUT THE AUTHOR

Julianna Slattery is a Christian psychologist and speaker in Akron, Ohio. She holds degrees in psychology from Wheaton College, Biola University and Florida Institute of Technology. Dr. Slattery has a passion for teaching biblical wisdom as it applies to everyday lives of women. She is a popular speaker and frequent guest on radio shows across the country.

To contact Dr. Slattery:

juli@drjuliannaslattery.com
www.DrJuliannaSlattery.com